WHAT NOT to do IN BUSINESS

Lessons Learned from Working at ~~Reputable~~ *Crappy* Companies

STEWART BARRON

ISBN: 061548994X
ISBN-13: 9780615489940

Contents

Introduction

We have all read the books showcasing supposed star companies. Those books are good if you happen to be in the lucky 5% that work for the truly successful companies. The remaining 95% of us tend to work in loser companies that are led by overpaid morons. We are the unlucky ones with the colleagues who make us wonder if they were the weird kids sitting in the corner eating glue in elementary school. I am like you. I have worked for nothing but bad companies. Instead of reading books about how great a select few companies are and rubbing it in your face, I think there is more to learn from reading about the mistakes of the losers. There is more to be learned from "what not to do."

Let's face it: most companies are not world beaters in business. They will never be. They will be like Goldilocks, not too good and not too bad. These businesses will be places where you don't mind hanging out for a few hours a day in order to get paid. Plus, you get the added perk of having birthday cake a couple of times a month without having to shell out a few bucks to buy anybody a gift. They will afford you a modest lifestyle and a glimmer of the good life upon retirement--assuming that you max out your 401(k) and the company doesn't go bankrupt first.

You will notice that most of this book has stories from the telecom and Internet industries. That is because those are the industries I choose to work in. It was actually not much of a choice—I took a temp job with a large telecom company during a recession to subsist after college. I parlayed that temp job into over a fifteen-year career. I have made good money working for mediocre companies throughout North America, the Caribbean, and UK. I honestly believe that I have worked with some of the best people in my industry; unfortunately, they were also working for companies that did not use them to their fullest abilities. A lot of these people went on to bigger and better things; many became CEOs of other companies or started their own successful businesses. It goes to show that they also learned a lot of important lessons on what not to do in business at the very same companies.

While a lot of the stories are based on my experiences in the telecom and Internet fields, I truly feel that they transcend industries and relate to almost all businesses. A lot of the stories and situations in this book were told to me by a number of people living it firsthand (dates, events, and company information were changed slightly to help disguise their true identities) and from a level to know the intricate details of the true stories, including the personalities behind them. There seems to be no shortage of material to learn what not to do. The only shortage I have seen is that of true leadership, individualism, and a long-term focus that is sorely lacking in today's business world. It seems that everyone went to the same business schools that taught the same ivory tower short-term thinking that leads to long-term issues. The concept of commonsense is surely not being taught or learned in business school or through on-the-job training. If it were, I would not have anything to write about. So, keep up the good work, overpriced Ivy League schools. I am sure there will be enough wackiness in the future to make truly entertaining stories for a second book.

In today's business world, we seem to reward mediocrity. I think it all goes back to human nature. We are all animals that seek the greatest rewards for the least amount of work (I guess I did pay attention in the Psychology 101 class my freshman year). Look around at the people that you work with.

Typically, one-third of the employees do 90% of the work. The next third of the employees do just enough not to get fired or cause anyone to notice their lack of effort. The last third should not even be there. Hell, the last third could not get up for a week and nobody would notice if it were not for an empty desk or lack of somebody to go around to get the birthday card signed for all the office birthday parties. The last bunch tend to be the same ones with the most company honorariums--from years of people kissing their asses to get them to actually do their jobs.

I remember working for a company one time where a President Award rewarded you with a check for $250. There was this one lady who absolutely sucked at her job. She was a bottleneck in marketing. Everybody had to run projects by her to get her blessing in order to put them on a marketing calendar so that they could be scheduled to be implemented. If she felt there was an issue, she could bog a project down until you either gave up or someone higher up overruled her. She was Queen Bee, and she knew it. This would not have been an issue if she were productive--she took cigarette breaks throughout the day that added up to almost half of her working day. Couple that with her personal calls, and she was lucky to get an hour a day of productive time.

I had a project that I felt was very important. I tried for weeks, going on months, to get it added to the calendar. I handled every one of her objections or requests for more information, but I could not succeed in getting it added to the calendar. My boss was asking me what was taking so long with the project. I should have had the project launched weeks ago. I finally broke down and told him what was happening. He suggested something I will never forget. He said to take some trivial thing that this lady had done that was slightly positive and make up some BS story about how this person really helped me and was a great asset to the company. Then submit it to the President's Award Committee. Sure enough, she got selected to receive the little trophy and cash reward; my project got scheduled later that week.

See, we reward mediocrity. Instead of firing this person, we gave her $250 for doing what she should have done in the first place as part of her normal salary. Now, I know what you are thinking. They should layoff the third of the people who should not be there. That is easier said than done. In the future chapters, I cover how some company managers have lists of who they will let go in the inevitable layoffs that seem to come around once every year. Hell, most of the layoffs companies do are not because business is bad––they just want to fire the slackers without a lawsuit! They have found it easier and cheaper to do mass firings than to document, provide warning, and then fire someone. The current process is too slow and fraught with lawsuits.

As businesses find ways to cope with unproductive workers, employees find ways to maintain jobs at poorly run companies. Beyond the traditional claims that unions protect unproductive workers, there are many non-traditional ways employees can hide and protect themselves. Some join committees or conveniently sign up for new projects with plenty of funding right before they are about to be let go. And some kiss enough ass that they get promoted. I think the latter are the type that eventually runs for city government.

I wrote this book as a way to help ordinary businesses minimize the mistakes that I am seeing all too often in businesses worldwide. Just think, if you could simply minimize the mistakes that 95% of today's companies make, you could become a rare thing in this world, a truly successful company. Please read the following book with a smile on your face. If you take this too seriously, you will miss the lessons. Experience is the best teacher, and what better way to learn than through the bad experiences of others?

CHAPTER 1

CEO 101

Being a CEO got a lot easier about ten years ago. Starting about that time, CEOs all started copying each other. I am not sure if they teach this specific class at Harvard or Wharton (places a lot of the S&P 500 companies' leaders went to school to learn to be "world-class business leaders." Yeah, I laughed at that statement, too). Instead of trying to be the best in the industry, it seems all that inspiring CEOs cared about was obtaining vast wealth. To obtain this goal, they needed a method to their madness. They discovered the Wall Street class, CEO 101.

CEO 101 is a step-by-step process of what to do when you parachute into a company you are clueless about running. It is for both the brand new CEO as well as the experienced option hopper (a term that I use to refer to CEOs who hop from company to company looking for the largest payout). It allows you to keep your board and Wall Street happy for at least two years until you can cash in your stock options before jumping to the next unsuspecting company. By the time everything has gone to crap, there will be another sucker, I mean CEO, in place to deal with cleaning up the mess. Besides, it was not your fault because you laid out the vision and the new CEO changed it to his or her vision, right?

The steps outlined are really geared to the ridiculously short-term thinking of public companies in the US and UK. Private companies typically do not go through such stupidity as Wall Street demands.

Step 1: Review the Parts of the Business

Have you ever wondered why a new CEO is not seen or the business does not seem to have changed in the first ninety to one hundred eighty days after he or she has taken over? CEOs usually have to move their families during the first quarter they come on board. This generates fat moving/relocation fees that give them a larger chunk to put down on houses in the best neighborhoods not too far from the company headquarters. During all this relocating, they have to actually create some type of plan for changing the business. They quickly get burned out. Imagine if your wife wanted to show you twenty homes over a couple weeks while you are trying to move to a new place, meet new people, and work eighty-hour weeks; you would get burned out, too. So what do you do to get away from the office and the wife without looking like a slacker who goes on vacation two weeks into the new job? You go and "review" all the operations around the world.

You get private jet service where you can get a good rest while flying (no screaming brats or fat guys who smell like sausage sitting next to you). You get to get out of having to be in the office from 7 a.m. to 8 p.m. You either get room service or meals out with the "best" customers. You can sleep in because you probably do not have any presentations before 10 a.m. Not a bad way to take an "at work" vacation with all expenses paid.

Nobody is every going to call you on this because you do technically need to see how the business works before you are knee deep in the muck. Only thing that sucks about step one is that you occasionally remember some of the people that you are meeting with will have to be laid off in step two. If you have a conscience, this is where the job begins to suck. If you have done this a few times, this is a great way to go on vacation.

Step 2: Layoffs and Stock Buybacks

The next steps are the layoffs, cost cutting measures, and stock buy-backs. The new CEOs do this because they know that they cannot affect the outcome of the business (if it is a decent size) for at least nine to twelve months. What board or Wall Street analyst does not love the idea of cutting costs and keeping near-term revenue stable? This translates directly to increasing the bottom line and thus the E in the Price Earnings ratio (PE); hopefully this will lead to a higher price for the stock. By combining this with less stock––due to stock buybacks––floating on the market and BOOM! The stock somehow magically rises. Pretty clever way of making it look like the new CEO is magic, when in reality it is totally short-term thinking that may or may not improve the future of the company.

The newly announced layoffs need to be in a quantity of greater than 5% but less than 20% of the total workforce. Why these numbers? If you layoff less than 5%, it appears that you are weak and are not an agent of change that is so desired on Wall Street. Layoff 20% or more, and Wall Street panics, thinking this is not just a simple turnaround but a possible bankruptcy situation. The latter is a surefire way of greatly reducing the value of the stock of the company, and thus hurting yourself in the options department. Like anything in life, moderation is widely accepted, and extremism is shunned.

As time has gone by, the announced layoffs and stock buybacks have become less and less effective. Investors (noticed that I did not say Wall Street, since in my mind, most of Wall Street is what you classify as dumb money with deep pockets) have started to notice that when CEOs are doing this, they need to watch their wallets because their pockets are about to be picked. I agree that there are times when this makes sense and needs to happen; in my opinion, a good 90% of it is done just to either prop up the stock or make the new guy or gal look good.

If the company was functioning well prior to the new CEO, and the new CEO does not have a strong history of success, wait for the pop-in stock price and then run for the exit. I have seen the charts that some on Wall Street have, showing the return in share price over the next twenty-four months after a buyback is better than increasing the dividend, but I personally feel that if you compared it over five years and show the inevitable decline, you would be better off with the dividend or the company reducing debt. Have you ever noticed how many times companies buy back their own stock at peak prices and do not have enough saved up for the tough times––that inevitably happen because of the business cycles––when they really should be buying back their own stock at the market lows? Imagine if all the banks had the cash that they spent in the early 2000s buying shares, in 2009, when everything had gone tits up. They may not have needed to be bailed out by the government.

Step 3: Create Your Vision

The new CEO should look for projects that have the potential for instant returns. No long-term projects. The CEO is stressing from the constant meetings with the board. The board wants to be sure they have the "right" guy. If they do not see the traditional spreadsheet graphs showing the hockey stick growth figures, they start looking for someone to replace the new CEO. This dictates that your vision needs to be eighteen months or less, even when you should be looking further out.

I am sure there have been some CEOs who had long-term visions who were let go twenty-four months into the change to only sit back and watch a new CEO step in and take the glory for the changes that they implemented but that did not have enough time to blossom. Unfortunately, this is how it typically goes in a normal or good economy. If you are hired in a recession and you have a long-term vision, you are golden. The down economy will buy you time to actually do what should have been done before. When the tide raises all the boats in your industry, yours will probably rise further because the changes were long-term in nature.

If you got thrown into a situation where the company is in trouble, you have to do something in the short-term or you will not be around long enough to cash in your stock options. Inevitably, you will have to create your own vision, but how? You probably have never had to really take something from nothing and build a business. Chances are, all that you have had to do was find the smart ones in your group and suck them dry for ideas to improve your department. The same thing can be done at the company vision level.

Look across your industry for someone who is truly revolutionary, someone like Steve Jobs (CEO and founder of Apple). Someone who does not care about what the world thinks of him or her and sticks to his or her guns and finds a new and innovative way of doing things.Chances are, you will not be able to duplicate them. It is simply not in your DNA. But what you can do is look at what they are doing and try to copy it and act like it is your idea. Just look at Microsoft. They make billions pulling this off every day. In my opinion, the Zune is a knock off of the iPod; the Xbox is an arguably better PlayStation, etc.

If you still do not think you are that talented, you can mimic famous dead people (coaches are always a favorite) or leaders from a different industry (everybody always wants to be a Steve Jobs). If that doesn't work, create an ambiguous mission statement.

Why an ambiguous mission statement? If you make it ambiguous, one of two things will happen. The first thing that you hope happens is that ten people read the same statement and get ten different ideas. You hope that one of these ideas will be good enough that you can latch on to it and ride it to option city so that you never have to work again. The second positive thing is that if it is ambiguous enough, people will not see that you are full of crap, and it will buy you time for the economy to improve in your favor. If the economy does improve, you can point to the mission statement to say it is because of your vision that you quoted sometime earlier. If the economy goes to crap, it is not your fault--it is the economy's fault.

Key Words and Phrases for Your Mission Statement

- **An industry leader**: Never "the" industry leader. "The" is too specific and measurable. Either you are the leader or not. "An" implies that you would be one of the top, but which one? Top 3, 5, 20––which one? That is the beauty of the ambiguous statement.

- **Broad industry types**: By this, I mean you paint with such a broad stroke that if one of the ideas that you are stealing from someone in your ranks turns out to be a gem, you can go for it because it is within your mission statement. To give you an example, instead of saying you want to be "the leader in mobile phone service in XYZ market," you say, "We want to be an industry leader in communications." The difference is that you might be good at only one niche, and you can still pull off your mission statement.

- **Add in the latest buzzword**: This is important because it makes you sound like you know what you are talking about without actually knowing more than how to read a *BusinessWeek* article.

- **Closing it with a shout out to the employees, shareholders, and other stakeholders**: This part is important because you want to get everyone's buy-in even if you really do not care. That way you look caring and compassionate, and step four is that much easier to do. Did you really think you would wuss out without a reason?

Example: Say you are the CEO of a company that makes ham for ham sandwiches (note to future authors: never write on an empty stomach).

Bad mission statement: XYZ corp. will be the industry leader in ham sandwich meat by 2012.

Good mission statement: XYZ corp. will be an industry leader in processed sandwich meats using synergies of an integrated supply chain to provide superior returns for our shareholders, while creating a great place to work for the benefit of our employees and the community at large.

There is nothing there that will get you fired. There is nothing that would offend or cause disagreement with the shareholders, employees, or the community. The statement insinuates growth and leadership without directly providing a measure or timeframe. In short, you basically just said a whole bunch of nothing. Your board, Wall Street, employees, and the community at large will love you for it. They will think you are the Superman of CEOs.

Step 4: Implement Your Vision

You had your ninety days of vacation "touring" all the company locations around the world. You have laid off a portion of your employees, so profits should be trending higher. You have started buying back stock, so this will help increase the company's earnings per share (EPS). Now it is time to implement your vision.

As part of your vision, all new CEOs must look at what portion of the business can be moved to China or India (some like to call it Chindia) to "save" money. Isn't that what the other CEOs are doing? If the other CEOs are looking to offshore to China or India, they must be saving money, aren't they?

China and India have this fabled reputation for cost savings. I do not have any stats on this, but my gut is that not all companies can benefit by offshoring jobs to China or India. I once worked for a company that moved its helpdesk to India. Being the 3,000,000[th] company to do so, they obviously did not have the pick of the litter when it came to employees. Working for the company in the US for a number of years, I knew the company had a reputation for paying low salaries everywhere they operated compared to most companies in that industry. I suspect they also did the same thing in India. Instead of getting bright and energetic staff at a fraction of the cost of an employee in the US, they got non-English-speaking, surly employees who typically quit every six to eight weeks to work for better-paying companies. You never worked with the same person twice even though the call center was staffed by less than fifty people. We had customers begging not to be sent to that call center. I am sure it cost us some customers. I am not convinced it really saved that much money, considering that the company had to train hundreds of people because the employee turnover was likely over 300% per year.

I have not personally worked with any companies offshoring to China. I suspect that they have a lot of similar issues. Let's face it. If you cannot successfully run a business and manage your employees locally, how much success will you really have with employees 10,000 miles away in different time zones? This is not a swipe at India or China, but unless you are well run like GE or IBM, this method of business will likely be more painful than it is worth. If you suck at home, chances are you will suck in China and India. Failure begets failure.

Let's get back to implementing our "Chindia" policy. You must get at least one trusted VP who will implement the strategy by looking to save money by offshoring. Here are the rules for identifying the right individual for the job.

- You cannot use a marketing VP because he or she will tend to create a mini-America with expensive new buildings and the Google-like coolness that permeates Google's headquarters. You will have nothing but a bunch of employees sipping lattes and playing video games instead of actually working. It will make a lot of press but add nothing to the company.

- You cannot get a customer service VP because, unless you already have employees working abroad, he or she will feel threatened that all customer service jobs will be sent overseas, including his or hers. He or she will purposely make the transition difficult at best, or virtually impossible.

- Ditto with hiring the head of the union because he or she will more than likely do the same as the VP of customer service.

- You cannot use a VP of engineering unless he or she is from those areas. If you use an engineer from the US, he or she will claim to be able to build a server or a robot that will do the job cheaper, because robots and servers are cooler than people. Engineers are weird like that. It is a different story if the engineer is from Chindia. He or she knows the culture and will probably be valuable in making it work. Chances are, the engineer will go back to his or her home country and live like a king because of the newfound importance in the community. Word of caution. You could also be creating a competitor who might kill your company, but what the heck––you only care about the next twenty-four months.

- That really leaves you with a VP from your finance team. He or she will probably do an outstanding job on keeping the costs down. On the negative side, they tend not to be able to see value, only costs. To counter this, get your VP of customer service over there once the paperwork has been signed and the build-out is started, and there is no way to change it.

So now we have our Chindia policy in place. This gives you the future layoffs in the US that you need in year two once the offshoring is up and sort of working.

Consultants and Organic Growth

During this step, it is also important to hire expensive consultants from large consulting companies. The larger the better. It is very important that the consultants come from places like Accenture, IBM, EDS, etc., and not companies like Harry's Discount Consulting Shop and Emporium. It is important to get a large name because this gives you deniability if things do not work out. You can always claim it was the large consulting company that gave you bad advice and not your own bonehead decision to follow it. If you employ Harry's consulting company to save a buck or two, you look like a moron that hired a second-rate firm, and the blame comes back to you. If things work out, you look like a genius that brought in the big guns to help sort out the mess from your predecessor. If they don't, you have another scapegoat.

These consultants will bring pretty graphs and some okay suggestions, and possibly will diagnose what is ailing your business. For a bonus, they will also sometimes give you ideas that you can use as your own for your vision on where the company should go. Hiring the consulting firm should give you enough ammunition with the board to allow you the latitude to force large changes in the company under the hope that it will lead to organic growth.

The next step in your vision is how to grow the company. This can be done one of two ways: organic growth or buying out a competitor. The hardest way is through actual leadership and hard work, or what business school calls organic growth.

Organic growth is the hardest to implement because it means your vision and direction are somewhat responsible for the growth. But, relax—there are two ways to get organic growth. The first way is through traditional means. You have to actually have a plan or at least good people under you who can deliver. If this is beyond your skills, don't worry—we have another way. The second way to get organic growth is through the old giveaway or discount method. Just because you have organic growth does not mean it has to be profitable. You can give away your service as a "trial" with the hope that it will grow into something that everyone uses, and then you can make money other ways (think Facebook, and forget all the other failures of once-hot companies like AOL, PointCast, Yahoo!, etc.).

I once worked for a large Internet company that gave away its service for free, or at a greatly reduced price, because it felt that it was more important to get "eyeballs on the network." "Eyeballs on the network" is supposed to mean that the company generates its revenue through ads sold to companies that wanted the exposure. The problem with this is that the company I worked for was an Internet Service Provider (ISP) that normally charged its end customers to get Internet access. This failed miserably, but hey, it took almost eighteen months before the company figured it out. That is just about as long as you need to cash in your stock options.

If organic growth is not possible (either by plan or through dumping your service for free), you can always do what 80% of the S&P 500 do and buy out a competitor. Buying out a competitor does three things. First, it eliminates some of your competition and could eliminate a well-run competitor before it gets too big and takes your company out. Second, your company spends money with large Wall Street firms who, in the past, tended to talk up your stock if you sent enough "advisory fees" their way. Finally, it makes it look like you possibly know what you are doing because some Wall Street analysts may take this as part of a rollup strategy.

Eliminating your competition is generally a good idea, provided you can do it at a reasonable price. The best way is by printing funny money, i.e., using your inflated stock. I call it funny money because the deal might have a high price tag to it, but you are actually paying for it by printing off your own shares. Remember how AOL was large enough to purchase Time Warner even though Time Warner earned billions while AOL had a history of losses? All AOL did was crank up the printing presses and produce more shares. The only money that exchanged hands was the Wall Street advisory fees and the bonuses and severance packages of some of the executives. The only way existing shareholders could get cash was by selling their shares. Now, if your competitor wants cold hard cash, make up some excuse why the deal fell through and move on before you are found out to be a fraud. Chances are, the company you were trying to buy is either run by someone who knew what he or she was doing, or the CEO owned a bunch of shares that he or she actually bought and wasn't given, unlike your shares.

Spending large sums with Wall Street firms used to be a surefire way of getting your stock on their "buy" list or on their "recommendation" list. These lists are where they give their unsuspecting retail customers ideas on what to invest in. Some of the time these pan out, but more than a majority of the time, these lists should be avoided like the plague. Please note that now Wall Street firms are supposed to have a Chinese firewall between their stock analysts and the investment bankers so this no longer happens. Whether this actually stops the practice, I am not sure. I do know that Wall Street is still recommending some poorly run companies that should never make any list except the "what to short because they are going to crash" list. So your guess is as good as mine.

You could also con--oh, I mean suggest--that this purchase is part of a bigger scheme where your company is buying out smaller competitors to gain efficiencies. This type of strategy is often called a rollup strategy. Rollup strategies can be effective if the industry is widely fragmented and efficiencies are possible by leveraging support roles like marketing, IT, customer service, and finance into one large company. A rollup strategy is where one company buys a lot of smaller competitors in the same industry so that it gains size and market share faster than it could with normal organic growth. This strategy is also used to build a national competitor in an industry that is highly fragmented with a bunch of tiny companies competing locally (example would be a company that buys up local dry cleaners across the country and labels them under one trade name). This was done effectively in the waste disposal and car dealership industries a little over a decade ago. An example of this is Waste Management. Waste Management has been effectively buying out smaller trash companies for years and wringing out inefficiencies through its centralized support network. For most industries this not possible, but that does not stop companies from trying. Sometime it feels better to be doing something rather than nothing.

Step 5: Claim Success of Your Vision if the Market or Economy Booms; Blame the Economy if the Results Suck

Your growth strategy has either been a success or you have miffed it. Don't worry—nobody will suspect that it was the economy that propelled your company to success. If you failed, hopefully the economy where you operate is also sputtering or failing, or your industry is going through a dry spell, because that is your get-out-of-jail-free card. See the common thread here. Heads you win, tails they lose. If the economy is crappy, hey, it's not your fault. If the economy is going great, then those changes that you made are working out. Only you (or some experienced managers in your industry) will know that you really did not do much. But what do you do if your company is going down while your industry is growing or the economy is doing well? You jump to step seven.

To tout your success and to help propel you into more lucrative future roles, or at least more options from your easily impressed board, you need to start doing media interviews. This is a very important step that should not be overlooked. The benefits are enormous. The first benefit is that you are getting your name in the public eye, and, like they say, there is no such thing as bad publicity. Next, you get treated like an expert in your field because you are actually talking to the press; they tend not to understand how a business is run anyway, so you can probably get away with it. In addition, prospective employers will now know your name as well as headhunters. The more times your name gets on their short lists for possible roles at other companies, the more money you can demand for your time and effort.

The key with doing the media interviews is to start small. Local newspapers where your business is headquartered are always a great place to start. They are happy to get the attention and will tend to write a favorable interview since it is seen as a positive for the local community in which they live. This is a great place to practice giving the all-important ambiguous answer.

It is not just a great strategy for politicians, it works great for CEOs as well. If you are unsure how this is done, spend some time with your local congressman or watch old tapes of interviews with President Clinton. In no time, you will be talking out both sides of your mouth without saying one thing that is too specific to come back and bite you in the ass. Remember, half the battle is stroking your audience, so spend some time reviewing past articles from your interviewer and speak highly of his or her writing. The reporter will be eating from your hands in no time.

After you have mastered the local press, you can move on to trade publications and press releases. These can be trickier since presumably the trade publications will know the industry well. You might want to bring your head of marketing to help with any difficulties that may arise. As these interviews get easier and easier, it is time to move into the big league, the national press. Before you get crazy and want to talk to the Wall Street Journal, the Economist, or CNBC, you need to spend a little time in the more bullish press. Start with magazines like Money or BusinessWeek. Both of those magazines are written for the novice investor, and 80% of their articles tend to say mostly good things about companies (with only one negative paragraph as the second to the last one) so as not to scare the new investors.

If you feel comfortable with the easier business publications, then jump to industry conferences put on by the brokerage houses and investor shows like CNBC and Bloomberg. The latter is a great way to tout your company with a short two-minute interview where the interviewer cannot really dig all that deep and ask tough questions. If you answer intelligently, you can really start to get people looking at your company. The industry conferences are an excellent way to get information about your company to brokers so that they can purchase your stock. Instead of being an interview, it is more of a presentation where you talk about the industry and things that your company is doing to lead it. In addition, sometimes the brokerage firm putting on the industry conference will put out a buy recommendation on your company since you are presenting (Wall Street will never admit it, but it does happen). This is a great way to get a short-term boost in share price. Now it is time to cash in your rewards for all this hard work.

Step 6: Cash in Stock Options if the Market or the Economy is Successful; if the World has Gone to Crap, Have the Board Reprice Your Options

So you have mastered the first five steps; now it is time for your reward. Hopefully when you negotiated your package eighteen months ago, you had a large portion in stock options. For those unfamiliar with stock options, let me give you a one-minute overview on what stock options are and how they work.

Stock options were designed to provide incentive for management to push really hard to get the price of a share of stock to increase. The board of directors issues stock options to upper management based on a strike price at today's price (backdating or looking back to give the option at a strike price that happened to be the lowest price of the year is illegal now). The board gives the managers a set number of options that represent a number of shares that they will award to the managers at a set price. Most boards make the options executable at a price equal to or greater than the current price so that the manager does not have to recognize the difference between the lower price and the current price as income the year they were written (i.e., pay taxes as a gain). This is because they know that options are for a period in the future and may possibly expire worthless. Typically, options are issued with a five- or seven-year expiration period. This is to avoid someone sitting on the shares until way in the future. Also, most options expire within ninety days of employment termination.

Management likes options because it is sort of like the lottery, where they can make a lot of money with no outlay of cash (i.e., they do not have to put any money upfront or pay any taxes on the options until they are exercised). To exercise an option, the manager puts in two simultaneous orders, one to exercise the options and one to sell the shares. That way they do not have to use any money upfront. The manager keeps the difference between the option purchase price and the price that they sold the stock for. Nobody would exercise an option that was for shares at a price higher than what the shares trade for on the stock exchange because they would lose money. If they wanted shares, they would simply buy shares on the open market and save money. Some managers use the options as a way to purchase shares cheaply to hold for a long time. That manager would pay the strike price times the number of shares purchased, *plus* pay taxes on the difference in price between the current price and the strike price.

If the stock market goes to crap, some managers will ask the board (off the record, of course) to reprice their options to a lower strike price. Sometimes the board will go along with the suggestion because it does not want to lose such "valuable" employees. This causes the managers to get a larger payday in the future. They only experience the upside, not any of the downside, if they owned the shares.

In my opinion, the only thing that options do is cause short-term thinking just to juice the price of the shares so that management can cash in the shares. They inflate CEO compensation and rob the corporation of the vital long-term thinking that is really needed to run a company right. I will save my rant for a later chapter.

An Example of How an Option Works

On January 1, 2009, XYZ corporation issues options granting one million shares at the current price of $25 per share to the new CEO. The options must be exercised by December 31, 2014, or they expire worthless. They can exercise some or all of their shares during the time up to December 31, 2014. Some companies also make a portion of the stock options only available based on length the employee have been with company. The company might make, say, only 20% awardable on every anniversary of the award (i.e., 20% on December 31, 2009, an additional 20% on December 31, 2010, etc.). For this example, we assume they are 100% vested on day one (i.e., they do not have to wait for an anniversary date to be able to cash them in, they can do it any time the stock moves higher).

On May 25, 2009, the stock price has gone up to $40 a share, and the CEO has a new Ferrari he is itching to buy, plus he wants to expand his summer home in the Hamptons. He decides to cash in 100,000 shares. He gets $15 (difference between the current price of $40 a share and the option price of $25) times 100,000 shares, or $1,500,000. He buys his Ferrari ($175,000) plus spends a further $825,000 fixing up the old summer retreat, plus pockets $500,000 to either pay taxes (probably from the tax year of 2003--he is a little behind), jet set, take a vacation, or pay his child support.

On January 1, 2010, XYZ corporation issues options for an additional one million shares to the CEO because things are going so well. The share price is now at $35. The CEO has two separate awards: a remaining 900,000 shares at $25 and an additional 1,000,000 at $35.

On April 15, 2010, the CEO decides to pay his back taxes for the last five years and needs some money. Unfortunately, the share price has declined to $30 per share. He needs $5 million to pay the taxes. So he sells 900,000 shares at $30 each and collects $4.5 million ($30 to $25 times the remaining 900,000 shares in the original award). He is still is $500,000 short. He cannot sell any of the second award because the strike price is lower than the current market price. If he executed the option, he would owe more than he makes selling the shares. This CEO will need to find the $500,000 from somewhere else; maybe he can bribe the board into giving him a bonus.

On September 15, 2010, the stock market crashes and the share price plummets to $8 per share. The CEO is panicking. He was counting on the option money to cover the cost of the villa in Aspen for the season ($200,000). He has no options that he can execute. So what to do? It is not *his* fault the stock price is so low; he cannot control the stock market. He proposes to the board to reprice his options to $5 per share because he is so valuable to the company. The board reluctantly agrees. He now has his way to pay for Aspen, and presumably the board has a happy CEO.

This is an oversimplification of how it works.

Step 7: New Round of "Cost Cutting" Because Vision is Not Working Out

This was bound to happen. The board is demanding a higher share price. You want a higher share price because you need a new Ferrari and your wife was complaining that your yacht was smaller than your neighbors' (think stock options). What to do, what to do? We tried out the vision, and it just does not seem to be making any difference. The vision was a great idea but the execution was lacking, yeah, that's what it was, the execution. "I would like to execute some of the people that work for me," the CEO thinks to himself as he wonders where he will get the money. "Always saying this will not work because of that. Hey, that gives me an idea--we have not had a round of layoffs in almost a year." And that is how it starts all over again.

There is an old saying, "Shit flows downhill." This is what economists in business schools like to refer to as the "trickledown theory." I kind of like the first. I think it is more appropriate. The CEO is being beaten up by the board and his wife. So he lashes out on the *little* people below him. He demands layoffs.

What board would reject a round of "cost cutting," i.e., layoffs? Throw in a buyback for your shares, and you have a winning combination. The board and your wife will get off your back for a while. Wall Street will love you because it looked like you listened to their analyst and you are going to give someone some trading fees for the buyback. It is the perfect solution until step eight provides you with a more permanent solution.

Step 8: Start Talking to Headhunters About New Positions With Other Companies

When all else fails or if you think the board is looking around to replace you, it might be a good time to dust off the old resumé. Dig deep in the Rolodex and look for the business card for the headhunter that placed you in the most recent gig. He or she was able to market you back then, so surely he or she can find something else for you now with all your additional experience. If you did step five correctly, you should have a known name in your industry. Headhunters will more than likely be calling you if you have met with moderate success or you happened to be lucky catching an up-cycle in your industry. If you totally miffed up the job, you can always bribe your board to let you go with a nice severance package in exchange for not cashing in those stock options or holding the company to your employment contract.

Once you have landed that new job, just start back at step one again. If you keep this up, you should amass a small fortune as long as you can avoid those messy divorces or sudden heart attacks that seem to befall a lot of our esteemed CEOs. Nothing sucks worse than spending twenty years working your butt off and selling your soul to see your money go to someone else to have a good time.

Lesson to Learn From This Chapter

A lot of this chapter is me being cheeky about the role of a CEO. To me, someone who has never been a CEO but has worked with a few, there seems to be a very similar pattern to how they operate. I feel these eight steps outlined above probably cover 80% of how most CEOs of public corporations in the US operate today, if they are not founding shareholders. Most CEOs probably do not realize that they are following this same pattern and honestly feel it is the best way to make a difference. I think if the CEOs stepped back and questioned all the silly short-term things that they do and tried to do something different, we would have a lot more successful companies. Just think––if companies stopped wasting their money on step two (layoffs and buybacks), they could save their companies absolute fortunes. Just in buybacks alone, if a company waited until the stock market was in a bear market to buy back shares, and saved the money when they were in a bull market, they probably could buy back 50% more shares. Even if they waited until the stock was trading at a fifty-two-week low, they could save a lot. Most stocks trade within a 30% to 50% range within a year.

CHAPTER 2

Rebranding a Pig

I had a friend who once worked for a company that had an image problem. They were a large telecom company that had literally been around since telephones were invented. They were (and in some cases still are) the monopoly in certain countries. They were seen as being an overpriced lumbering giant. They had a habit of taking days to restore service when there was an outage. They had software and systems that were over twenty years old and required a lot of manual intervention, possibly divine intervention, to exorcise the demons that existed in their servers. Customers hated to deal with them and dreaded the long lines in the retail stores and the even longer hold times calling their customer service number.

Every market survey or focus group that was conducted showed the company in poor light. The only things the company had going for it was that it had a solid engineering staff and had majority market share in the markets where it operated. The solid engineering helped the company maintain an okay image for quality of the underlying service, but if you needed a new service or repairs to an existing service, it could literally take weeks. Their bills routinely had errors where customers were over- and undercharged. The saving grace for the company was that it had been able to maintain a leading market share even after its monopoly was removed by the local government. The board of directors of the company recognized they had a problem, and if they did not change things soon, they would be toast. Not having a solid leadership team, they decided to bring in outside experts to help them out.

The lethargic company hired a pricy CEO from outside the company, who had a history of leading other companies in the industry as they transitioned from a closed market to one with full competition (at least that is how it was portrayed). His arrival at the company caused tension in the community and at the company. The community did not like the idea that a non-local was running the largest telecom company in the country. The company managers resented that nobody from their ranks was chosen to lead and the fact that the new CEO tended to look down at the locals.

So what do new CEOs do after they go through the first phases of CEO 101? That's right—they go right to the expensive and worthless consultants of the world to get "fresh ideas." As you probably guessed it, the consultants who were brought down from the US to this "backwater" country (not my term, theirs) were not the cream of the consulting crop. The best consultants in the US tend to go to three areas: Wall Street, DC, and Silicon Valley, where they can maximize their income and reputations. The consultants who tended to go to where this company was located were either fresh out of college and looking for an adventure or they were failed corporate executives who were just trying to pay their mortgages while they waited for a real job to open up in their field.

The consultants all flew down to the country on business class tickets. They stayed in the nicest resorts. They ate at the finest restaurants. They drank the best wine. Some even brought their families as some sort of vacation. All the while, the company paid these consultants tens of thousands of dollars per month. Most of the consultants worked two weeks in the country and one week out of the country. This went on for at least six months.

To recap, you have a highly compensated executive and consultants with little local market knowledge designing the company change procedures for markets where they might have only ever visited while on vacation. In short, they did not have a clue about what to do. All they did was work and party. They spent a lot of time talking to people. They spent a lot of time creating PowerPoint after PowerPoint presentation. And then came the time to recommend their changes.

Their recommendation was for the company to change its name and spend a lot of money on a marketing campaign to try to influence its customers' opinions so that they would think the company was a good one. Instead of using the old company name, they recommended a clean slate where a new company name was introduced without the legacy baggage of the historically poor service. Very little was said about actually fixing the underlying problems. They felt that if they created slick ads showing local people working for a company with a new and fresh image that *appeared* to be that of a well-run company with modern systems and good customer service, you would not *actually* need to have those things. When my friend told me about this, I was shocked. Basically, the concept was to trick the customers into thinking that their actual experiences were not happening and that this illusion was reality. The consultants even went so far as to have a calculation of the cost of the campaign based on the number of times (touches, in marketing speak) a customer would need to hear or see their ads to change their opinions of the company. The cost of the campaign was almost $10 million. Ten million dollars would have gone a long way in fixing a lot of their internal issues.

The CEO thought it was a great idea. The board, not wanting to seem ignorant, agreed with this CEO and placed him on a pedestal as some type of management god that was going to save their poorly run company.

So the board and CEO *wisely* decided to change the name of this company that has been known in the market and around the world for over a hundred years. In addition, they coupled that *brilliant* decision with the notion to have a reorganization and reduce the number of employees by 30% (obviously an idea from a consultant) to address the slow response rates and poor systems. "Problems solved," the CEO thought; he could cash in his options and sit back and have a cool rum drink under a coconut palm tree on the beach.

But the problem was not solved. You can't fix companies that are poorly run by changing company names, running a slick ad campaign, and laying off people. You need to do the hard work. You need to invest time in training, purchasing newer automated equipment, and fixing the broken processes. In short, you cannot do more with less without first spending a little time addressing the problem. Wasting money on slick campaigns to brainwash customers into thinking that you have a good company is just plain ridiculous. I would go so far as to say it was borderline criminal given the fact the company was facing increased competition as more and more competitors entered its markets. The competitors were entering the markets because they felt they could easily take market share from the poorly run dinosaur.

My friend left that company shortly after it was announced it was changing its name. He did not want to be anywhere near that company when the train wreck hit. For consultants who rely on their good names in the industry, being part of a disastrous business decision like changing the company name and not fixing the problems can quickly ruin a reputation. Even if my friend did not work directly on the name-changing project, he was guilty by association. Just ask people who worked for Enron or Bear Stearns how hard it is to get a job immediately after those debacles happened, even if they were top in their fields.

More Name Changing – What do you call Junk?

Back in the early 80s, there was this smart and aggressive trader of bonds by the name of Michael Milken. Milken worked for the infamous New York investment bank Drexel, Burnham & Lampert. Milken had discovered that not many investment banks would put together financing deals to help non-investment grade companies (risky companies with questionable ability to repay the loan) sell bonds. There was clearly a need for these speculative companies to issue debt to expand their businesses or acquire competitors. He discovered that there was an appetite for these high-yielding bonds on Wall Street from pension and insurance funds that wanted a little more yield. He almost singlehandedly created the market for junk bonds as we now know it today. His encouragement to get companies to buy these bonds led to a sudden increase in liquidity in this once-shunned part of the bond market.

With liquidity come more people interested in the market. Then, when things start really heating up, Wall Street starts getting greedy. Banks and investment firms throw billions of dollars at suddenly hot markets, hoping to make a quick buck and leave before everything crashes. Milken noticed the market that he helped nourish from its infancy grow to such heights that greed started to set in. He wanted to bring to market more bond offerings so that he could make larger profits and take home bigger bonus checks. To keep feeding this machine, he needed two things: supply and demand. Demand was taking care of itself. People and companies were getting rich selling this debt, leading to a large growth in demand for these debt issues. Supply was the problem. Back in the 1980s, companies were a little more conservative than they are today. There were only so many companies that wanted to take out debt with yields in the 10% to 18% range. Milken noticed he was constrained on the supply side of the equation. In a fit of wisdom, he recognized that some aggressive traders/raiders were willing to pay these high yields if the bonds helped them finance takeovers of cash-rich companies. These "leveraged buyouts," as they were called in the 80s, were the game for the aggressive traders/raiders. The raiders felt that the lower the equity they had in a deal, the better the return they could get for their investors. It also allowed them to stretch their equity, allowing them to purchase bigger and bigger companies. Like a snowball rolling down the mountain that becomes an avalanche, these deals feed on each other with raiders trying to outdo their "competition" and have bragging rights that they made the largest deal.

Wall Street falls over itself to get market share in a growing market. Banks and investors were spending money like drunken sailors on leave after nine months at sea. Greed and stupidity were not too far away. Sooner or later, this will lead to the crash of the market. Stupidity, greed, and money tend to have a multiplying affect. Beyond normal greed is outright corruption and illegal trading that also seems to always find its way into the fray when stupid money is about. So under the weight of greed, corruption, and stupidity, the market for junk bonds and leveraged buyouts crashed in the late 80s, only to rear its head during the Internet boom of the late 1990s and the housing bubble of the 2000s.

In the mid-1990s, Wall Street wised up and realized that they would never be able to sell it to their shareholders that they were once again playing in the junk bond market and working with leveraged-buyout firms. So they spun it and simply renamed them. Instead of trading in junk bonds, they traded in "non-investment grade bonds." Instead of putting money with leveraged-buyout firms, they now put their money with "private equity" firms. I like the latter name change. Instead of sounding overleveraged, with a name like leveraged buyout, they now sound like they are investing in equities, with private-equity firms. Same shit, different name. There must be a public relations firm that specializes in finding less offensive names.

Changing a name to Build "Trust" (Fund)

Social Security was (and still is) a pay-as-you-go system. A pay-as-you-go system is where current revenue (taxes) are collected, to pay out benefits to people today that the people accrued in the past. This is very similar to a Ponzi scheme, where early investors are paid out of proceeds from the new investors. Like a Ponzi scheme, pay-as-you-go systems usually implode from the weight of future demand for money "invested" previously. This type of system only works in the long term if the rate of return of the investment is low and the future demand is lower than the current intake of revenue (taxes). It all falls apart when they have to pay out more than they can handle. In 1983, the Social Security Administration recognized that it was on a path to ruin, so it decided to kick the proverbial can down the road to future generations. It raised the current tax (increased revenue) and raised the retirement age (lowered future demand). This resulted in more revenue being collected for the giant Ponzi scheme. Congress, being Congress, saw extra revenue in the government coffers and started spending it. To "account" for the government dipping its grubby hands in what some people would classify as retirement savings, it created a "trust fund."

My guess is that the Department of Treasury must have hired the same PR firm as the investment bankers did for junk bonds to help address the Social Security issue. To cover up the fact this really is a tax to help lower the current deficit, the Department of the Treasury spun the tax as a "trust fund" that purchases Treasury bonds to fund the future retirement for the people who did not save enough of their own money for retirement. That is similar to me writing an IOU to myself and putting it in my piggy bank and treating it like real savings. If I try to spend those IOUs at the corner store, I would probably get my ass kicked by the owner. Nice try, Treasury, but come on, calling it a trust fund is just going a little too far. Only thing you can trust is that it will not be there when you need it most. As I write, Social Security owes future obligations of $14 trillion. Add this to the Medicare problem (same as Social Security, but bigger), and we are in a world of trouble. You better start saving!

Lesson to Learn From This Chapter

In my opinion, all these situations are the equivalent of putting lipstick on a pig. It might be a prettier pig now, but at the end of the day, it is still just a pig. Businesses should look to fix their issues (at least their serious deficiencies) first before trying to be too cute with marketing or growing business out of the problems. If business executives today sat down and said, "I want to be at X place in three years," and then asked themselves what needs to get done to get there, they would have a plan. They would know what needs to be fixed because it is vital to the future direction of the business. Instead, they bounce around from trend to trend and, at best, are moderately successful. Even if they are successful for a short period of time and they did not have a plan, they have no idea how they got to their goal. They do not know what made them successful or how to keep the positive uptrend going. In the end, the initial success for somebody without a plan will more than likely meet up with failure. In the real world, luck runs out, but planning and perseverance usually win out. That is why great managers are like good coaches--they teach and stress the basics, and they always have a plan.

CHAPTER 3

Six Sigma, Matrix Management, and Other *Fine* Management Systems

"There are two times in a man's life when he should not speculate: when he can't afford it, and when he can."
-Mark Twain
"The three 'I's:' First come the *innovators*, who see the opportunities that others don't. Then come the *imitators*, who copy what the innovators have done. And then come the *idiots*, whose avarice undoes the very innovations they are trying to use to get rich."
-Warren Buffett
"Be fearful when everyone is greedy. Be greedy when everyone is fearful."
-Warren Buffett

Why did I quote these two great American characters (one in literature and one in business) that are often associated with business books? Because it instantly gives me credit with my audience. Nobody is going to doubt these two individuals. Their history is rock solid. Quoting them gives credence to my writing. Most business books use quotes to do just that. If the author is an unknown writer or the message is somewhat weak, he or she can strengthen it by quoting true leaders and original authors to boost the validity of the message. Now *why* am I really doing this? To prove a point.

The same thing happens in the world outside of business books. It happens with our CEOs. Most CEOs are not really that talented; in fact, most of them are flying by the seats of their pants. I know that comes as a shocker, but it is true. What they did learn is the art of selling (some say BSing). They sell themselves to the board, Wall Street, and their employees as being top leaders. One way to accomplish this is by mimicking people who are much smarter than they are. If they hear that GE is using a certain management system, then it must be a good system. To attack the CEO about his or her plans to use the same system that GE is using is to attack GE itself. In short, mimicking a top-ranked company gives the CEO street credit for his or her proposed management system even if he or she really miffs it up.

The CEOs who do not like to do the steps outlined in CEO 101 and want to really help their companies, or are simply lost, sometimes read books about management systems in order to improve their own businesses. Most humans are followers. They are not leaders or truly that unique. The ones who are, are in high demand. Like the Warren Buffet quote above, there are very few innovators (See how I worked in credibility to my writing? Thanks, Warren for the use of your street credit. I should be careful—anytime Warren extends credit, he expects to be paid ☺). Simply, most companies do not have the budget or need for this top talent.

A perfect example of a management system is Six Sigma. Six Sigma is a management system Jack Welch used in running GE, to great fame. It was originally deployed at Motorola (see, everybody copies each other). Six Sigma is similar to TQM (Total Quality Management), where you try to identify defects in your service or products and eliminate them so that you strive to have an error-free product or process. It takes its name from the number of standard deviations that a company works to get to, to be error free. Each deviation from the normal operation improves the chances for a successful result (i.e. very little errors). Six Sigma is supposed to represent 99.9997% error-free (thank you, Wikipedia, for that). This means Six Sigma goal is to be practically error free. If you can get a business to be practically error free in its operations you can save vast sums of money and time while improving your customers' experience. Six Sigma differs from TQM because TQM was really just for manufacturing whereas Six Sigma actually looks beyond just manufacturing and looks to improve business processes as well. In Six Sigma, the company trains "Black Belts" to be resident experts at processes, products, or programs. These experts are supposed to help a business achieve continuous process and product improvements to thus deliver predictable results. In short, like all good management systems, it is a way to lead a company in one solid direction so that everybody knows what their role is and how to improve the business. This is the 30,000-foot academic view. In reality, the only way these systems work **and** keep working is if they become part of the core culture (some use the buzz word DNA) of the company. The minute the company loses focus, the system starts to deteriorate.

Six Sigma and TQM are fine systems if the company employing them is a well-run company. Some would like to say that Six Sigma and TQM can take a bad company and make it good. I tend to disagree. It is the leader who really can turn the business around. And it is that leader who will deploy quality management systems to help the process. The processes cannot take a second-rate leader and make him or her first rate. Only education, determination, and experience can do that.

I feel some of the success or fame of a management system also relies on how close the CEO is to other CEOs who have been the innovators of a particular management system. TQM works so great in Japan because William Deming worked directly with many companies there to continuously help improve their products. I would guess a similar thing happened between Jack Welch and the CEO from Motorola with Six Sigma. I am saying this because I feel (i.e., my opinion) that the 2% to 5% of the CEOs who deploy the system are close enough to the innovators to help deploy the system correctly. In addition, if you are in touch with high-caliber CEOs, more than likely you tend not to be that much of a slouch yourself (i.e., you are probably a good leader already). Like anything else, people with similar occupations, talents, and hobbies tend to gyrate toward like people. The other 95% of the CEOs get their information passed to them by consultants, books, periodicals, TV, or word of mouth. That is where the problem lies.

The other 95% of the CEOs get their ideas from going to Barnes & Noble and perusing the $1 book tables of old books in the discontinued pile. They then proceed to buy whatever twenty-four-month-old "revolutionary" management technique book they happen to scrounge up. Or, if the CEO is a little more current and can read above the *Dr. Seuss* level, he or she gets the idea from *BusinessWeek* or *NY Times* book reviews. Then they actually make a trip to a bookstore to seek this book out so that he or she can try to implement it at the company to improve on poor performance. Or even worse happens.

CEOs, like other people, are always looking for a quick fix to long-term problems. Like an overweight person looking for the next miracle diet, the CEO is always looking for the next miracle management system that will improve the business. The danger starts when the do-good CEO is having a bad quarter. He or she knows what is happening today is a symptom of a deeper problem––the company is being run poorly or it is in a need of a change. Innocently enough, the CEO travels to a location to see other operations, customers, or whatever gets a CEO on a flight these days. The flight is delayed or there's a long layover. The CEO decides to peruse the airport because he or she is bored. He or she discovers the Barnes & Noble or another bookshop, deciding to stop in. And there it is. An answer to the company's problems. The latest self-help book for corporations, announcing a new management system that helped X corporation to turn around and become a world leader.

Did you notice what all these things have in common? CEOs are not innovative enough to create their own systems, so they plagiarize it off of another company that is successful. This is not restricted to management techniques. Look at a lot of the Japanese and Korean luxury cars. They are almost direct knock-offs of Mercedes Benzes, if they were built in the late '90s or of BMWs if they were built in the mid-2000s. The Japanese and Koreans are great businesspeople, but when it comes to original design, they are like the rest of us, more misses than hits. To propel their luxury brands, they mimic already accepted style and improve on quality and price. I suspect that future generations of the Japanese and Korean cars will lead in design, but the initial couple of product runs were meant to get the brand accepted and build market share; the next will be for leadership of the luxury market. Now, some may knock them for copying designs. All I can say is at least they never designed the Pacer. It shows even they know when to copy something and when to let it be.

Why Six Sigma Sucks

It is not so much the management system (excluding Matrix management, which does truly suck, as I will explain later) as it is the company executing the management system that sucks. Most companies deploy the system hot and heavy for a month or two, hoping that it will fix an otherwise poorly run company. The management system never truly becomes part of the core mission; it becomes an afterthought or a chore, not a solution.

First off, it sucks for employees because of two reasons. The first reason is that nobody who is decent at his or her job usually has the time to go to the classes and do the steps that it takes to make it work. This is especially true since employees realize that more than likely the new management system will die a slow death over the next six to nine months. Why spend the effort and deal with the distractions when it will all be for naught?

The second reason it sucks for employees is that the only people who have the time are the two-thirds of the staff who are not the overachievers. The two-thirds who do have the time either do very little or nothing, and they realize taking these classes and going to these meetings are a great way to take an on-the-job vacation. Camping out in some conference room for a day is a great distraction from actually having to do any work. They have their convenient excuse to not do their jobs (as if they needed one before). In addition, what also tends to happen is that one or two of these people get appointed as the department lead of this new system.

The people who get put in charge of implementing the management system in their departments tend to let the power go to their heads. They always seem to be the middle-aged fat guys that nobody knows what they do for the company, outside of celebrating everyone's birthday or holidays just to get the free cake. They quickly become the management systems Nazis.

To celebrate their newfound power, they like to hold big meetings that are mandatory to attend in conference rooms. They bore you with regurgitated slides from a presentation that they received from a Black Belt (Six Sigma) or some other teacher higher up. They barely know what the information on the slides means. They read every word on every slide since they do not know enough to ad lib. Ask them a serious question, and you will stump them for hours.

As a side note, it is sometimes fun to try ganging up on them with a couple of your office buddies with a bunch of difficult questions to make them really look like they don't know crap. Pretty soon everybody in the room will be questioning why the company is going to this new management system.

I personally usually try to duck out of these meetings when the power goes way too much to their heads and they want to do stuff like turn the conference room into a mini concentration camp for the new employees and any temps that may be lying around. The only good thing that ever comes from power plays like this is that the "newbie smell" quickly gets rubbed off from the new employees. It also tends to take the twinkle out of the eyes of the "fresh from business school twenty-somethings."

Matrix Management

This is the only management system that truly sucks. I am not aware of any company that has successfully used this system over the long run (i.e., greater than twenty-four months) to great success. This management system keeps getting recycled through the list of newest and greatest management systems once a decade or so. Sometimes I think management consultants have a list of five or six management systems they try to sell to companies as the latest and greatest system. Every twenty-four months, they seem to change their recommendation just to get more consulting fees. They add a few new components and change the names, but basically they are the same systems that failed in the past.

Matrix Management must have been designed by a college professor or CEO without any common sense. All they saw was an opportunity to **theoretically** save money. How Matrix Management is supposed to work is common resources are shared among multiple "bosses" or teams. Example is product development engineers. Instead of having one for each product, they have a couple covering multiple products. Sometimes Matrix Management is also deployed when a company wants to share resources across multiple countries to save costs. This is, in theory, an efficient management system. In practice, it causes areas in the organization where bottlenecks in productivity occur on a regular basis.

Matrix Management sucks for the simple reason that it never works to have multiple bosses. Answering to multiple people is like having multiple wives (unless you are Mormon and are used to the drawbacks). There is either way too much nagging or very little concentration on one thing just because you are trying to keep too many people happy at once. What usually happens is one of two things. Either all your bosses want your full attention to their projects or they totally leave you alone thinking you must be swamped from all the work from other bosses. So that means the employees are either extremely overworked and become a bottleneck for the company, or they do not have anything to do but cruise the Internet on company time and pick up a paycheck for doing so. You can usually spot the former from the latter. The former gets in at 6:00 a.m. and leaves at 8:00 p.m. only to VPN to the companies servers at home an hour later. Their hair starts to fall out and they gain twenty pounds in what seems like only one month.

The latter always has time to always make a Starbucks run or send around funny emails.

Lesson to Learn From This Chapter

The lesson from this chapter is simple. It is not the management system that is deployed, it is the management team deploying it that's important. Successful companies like GE would have been successful even if they never launched Six Sigma. Arguably, Six Sigma helped propel them into an entirely different league of successful company. Jack Welch would have found another management system and probably would have been just as successful as with Six Sigma. The reason is GE has spent time and effort building up its culture of success for an extremely long time. I hate to use this term, but "success is in their DNA." That does not mean that GE cannot fail. It just means that GE has enough professional managers who truly know how to run a business that it would take a long time for them to start on a path to destruction. Remember, General Motors used to be a world-class company way up until the early 1970s. They took their eye off the ball and started down a path that eventually led to bankruptcy in 2009. It took almost forty years for them to fail totally, i.e., go bankrupt. For GE to go down that path, I think it would probably take about the same amount of time because they have a habit of continuously promoting from within, always looking for the best talent. Now, I will stop kissing Jack Welch's butt and move on to the next chapter.

CHAPTER 4

Incredible IRR for Business Cases Just to Make It Through Financial Review

This chapter might come as shock to some economists, but there is really a type of inflation they never teach you in college. Typically you learn about inflation, deflation, stagflation, asset inflation, etc. in your macro-economics class. The professors all claim to know what causes each one of these phenomena to exist. I have a new type of inflation––never discussed or even anticipated in business school. It is called "business case inflation."

Business case inflation is true inflation because it affects demand for underlying products and services that a business purchases to produce its end product or service. Business case inflation works like this. Either a board or CEO restricts capital for new projects or they simply insist that growth of the business match anticipated future growth in their industry. This causes the next few layers of management to react by changing their business cases to meet management's new "norm." They either have to show outrageous returns if they are restricting capital or they have to show outrageous growth to meet the CEO's or board's industry growth expectations. The former leads to lottery-like paybacks and cash flow projections, the latter leads to the familiar hockey stick growth projection charts that project everybody on the planet will have your gizmo by sometime early next year. In short, the

CEO or the board is asking the people below them to lie, sorry, stretch the truth about their projects just to get them through management review. The sad part is the CEO or the board honestly thinks they are doing the smart thing by choosing the most outrageous business cases with impossible returns just because it could potentially make them look good. They are gambling the company's future instead of investing in it.

Business case inflation can be best illustrated in the following example of WorldCom. In the late 1990s, WorldCom claimed to have demand for its Internet services growing at over 100% per year. Other telecom companies were generally seeing high growth but not to the same high levels that WorldCom was claiming in press releases and at conferences. They were seeing growth in the double digits (generally 20 to 40% per year). It was still rapid growth, just not as rapid as WorldCom was supposedly experiencing. The different boards of directors and Wall Street analysts were asking the CEOs of the other Internet companies why they were not growing as fast as WorldCom. Instead of questioning WorldCom's results, they were questioning other companies' results. Some of the CEOs hit on the idea that their reason for their poorer performance was lack of cheap bandwidth. The only way to make the cost of their network cheaper was to scale up their network capacity. The more bandwidth that was added to the overall network, the cheaper per Mbps the network got. The CEOs pushed back and used this claim to get approval for business cases with costs in the billions of dollars to expand their existing networks to meet the "industry demand."

The race was on. It seemed like all the companies in the telecommunications industry were trying to up themselves on the size of their networks. At first they were bragging about OC-3 (a measure of capacity that stands for Optical Carrier third level, which is the equivalent of 3 DS3s or 155 mbps). Then it became OC-16, then OC-48, and finally OC-192 (equivalent of 10 Gbps of capacity). This boom in network construction caused a lot of the inflation that was seen in the late '90s. This caused fiber optics, network equipment, engineers, product managers, you name it, as long as it was associated with Internet, to bid up to sky-high levels. This growth in demand for anything Internet-related led to large salary growth in unrelated industries in Washington, DC, Silicon Valley, and Seattle as local companies tried to compete against Internet firms that were hiring anybody with a pulse. The resulting areas saw large growths in populations that caused the local prices for real estate, gym memberships, restaurants, anything thing people do or consume, to reach crazy levels. This also led to some knock-on inflation in U.S. government salaries, and thus everyone's taxes, because a lot of the U.S. governments' main offices happen to be in Washington, DC. I personally saw my salary increase fourfold within five years as I climbed up the ladder and took on more responsibility within some telecom companies that were rebranded as Internet companies.

All of the growth in capacity was based on the false assumption that growth would continue indefinitely and that the other companies had to catch up to WorldCom. It was later discovered when WorldCom went bankrupt that a lot of their growth numbers were made up to keep their share price high. This growth in networks was unsustainable and caused a lot of carriers to file bankruptcy and prices for bandwidth to plummet as more and more network capacity hit the marketplace, flooding the U.S. and parts of the world with too much supply.

This could have been avoided if two things had happened. First, if the people approving the business cases had stopped and used common sense, they would have seen there was simply too much growth in capacity. The growth in capacity outstripped demand multiple times over. This problem persists today, more ten years after many of these networks were completed. A similar thing happened in the banking and shadow banking industries where too much credit was offered to purchase houses and stuff to fill the houses. Very few people are truly leaders and have the guts to question where they are headed. If they did, bubbles like that would not happen.

The second thing that could have been done is a total contrarian move. They could have sold their network assets to another company and leased back what they needed. Then when the companies went bankrupt, they could have purchased the assets at a fraction of their construction costs. As

I write, the same thing is happening in housing. People are purchasing new or relatively new houses at discounts of up to 70% off the price that was paid in the housing bubble. I personally have benefited from this. I purchased a two-year-old house for about 45% of the cost of construction, just down the street from my old house. Not that I am some type of financial genius, I just happen to know a good deal (read: I am a cheap bastard). It also stopped my wife complaining about the size of my old house (read: I am trying to keep my wife happy even though I am a cheap bastard).

Personal Example of Bad Business Case Approvals
The Shiny Box Business Case

I once worked for a unit of a large international telecom company that had a big legacy problem; they were strong in engineering. Now some may question what is so wrong with being strong in engineering. Let me explain. Engineers (telecom, electrical, chemical, it does not matter) think new technology is cool, and to them status is having the newest technology (i.e., toys) on the block. In short, they think it makes them look cool. Some call this the "shiny box syndrome." How can this impact the firm? Let me explain. The location where I worked happened to be located on a wealthy tropical island that was devastated by a major hurricane (Category 5 with gusts over 210 mph). It totally leveled the island. After the storm, power was not restored to most homes and businesses for almost four months. The company had to bring in line crews to restore telephone and Internet service (from the U.S.). It took almost six months for them to rewire the entire country. If you were not an engineer or a network operations member, you were flown to Miami to work remotely to ease the strain on the destroyed infrastructure on the island since because of the limited power, water, and food.

A storm that size brings some benefits. The major benefits are the insurance money and the ability to upgrade legacy systems to more current technology. For the engineer, it is the worst of times and the best of times all rolled into one. They had to work incredibly long hours for weeks at the time, but they got to choose the new toys they got to play with. And man, did they choose! They knew they were due over $100 million from insurance. So they spent like drunken sailors that were given only a twenty-four-hour R&R pass after being at sea for six months.

This led to the engineers wanting to experiment with the latest technology. Someone got the brilliant idea that they would try to roll out WiMax in a limited area (about half the island). WiMax is basically mobile phone technology on steroids. It is a high-speed data network that you can use for data, Internet, or voice calls over the Internet (VoIP). In theory, it was a sound suggestion. Instead of spending millions of dollars rolling out a copper or fiber optic network, all you would need to do would be mount receivers on cell towers throughout the area where you were restoring service. The trouble was that the insurance companies only wanted to repair existing infrastructure and not pay for the company to use technology to leapfrog into a more advanced network. So, to compromise, the telecom company agreed to spend a little over $1.5 million on the new solution. That is great, but the new technology had a cost of $2 million for a turnkey solution to meet the company needs.

The company went back to the supplier and asked if they could break down the costs so that they could choose what they really needed and what they could do without. This is where the limited number of people on the island kicks in. Normally, the different groups in the company (engineers, marketing, billing, etc.) would get together in this type of situation and jointly decide what could be cut and what had to stay. In this situation, only the engineers were present. They decided they only needed the receivers, network servers, and spares, but did not need the billing, ordering, and customer service software. Hey, they are engineers--what do they care if the company can bill, order, or support customers? They only cared that they had the latest technology. In their minds, the solution worked. You could cruise the Internet, make calls, or send data. Great, but how do you sell a solution that you cannot support in a service industry? The engineers never even considered that to be an issue.

So time goes by. After almost one year, things were about 90% back to normal. All employees were back and performing their normal roles. Customers were back up to 90% of their pre-hurricane service demand levels. They had a new network in place. The management started asking why the business case for WiMax wasn't producing any revenue yet. Marketing, billing, and customer service all said they couldn't use the current solution because they didn't have the tools to perform their roles. Management then started asking the tough questions. They decided to ask the supplier to give them a new quote for purchasing the software and support systems (servers and integration support, mainly) for the existing solution. The supplier notified them that technology had improved so much with WiMax that they were no longer rolling out the same solutions and no longer offered an off-the-shelf solution for the system that they implemented. For them to do it now would be an ad hoc request and would cost the company around $1 million more, double what it cost just a year before. The company balked at the steep price tag and decided to use their engineering staff and consultants to write some code that would integrate the WiMax solution into their current billing, ordering, and customer service solutions.

After six months and about $250K worth of consultant time trying to make the WiMax solution integrate with their billing system, they decide to pull the plug because the solution was rapidly becoming out of date. It would have taken probably another $200K to finish the project. The problem was that newer WiMax technology was becoming widely available at a cheaper price. Just in the eighteen months that they had been playing with the solution, speeds and the speed of data that could be sent had advanced by almost four times. Cost had also come down for the networking kit. They could now purchase four times the capacity for about half as much as they did less than one and a half years prior. They sold off the old system for pennies on the dollar and decided to try again.

This time, all the groups got together and spec'd out a complete solution. The price tag came to $1 million, but a new problem lurked: finance. The finance department did not want to spend $1 million dollars so soon after the first business case failed so miserably. Finance would only approve $800K. The last I heard, they were asking the supplier to break down the cost. I wonder if they ever bought the support systems the second time around?

Impossible Returns Business Case

This next example shows business case inflation pretty clearly. It also shows that boards of directors and management want impossible returns on projects they know they need to implement to stay relevant in their industry.

I was working for a large telecom firm in the U.S. that was looking at expanding its web hosting business since it was approaching full capacity at its existing two data centers. Management and analysts predicted that they would be at 100% capacity within twelve months based on current company **and** industry growth rates. The data centers were large money-makers for the telecom company. They sold rack space, IP and data capacity, as well as advanced IT services to a number of their top clients. It allowed the company to climb the proverbial food chain with clients and become entwined with their IT management and thus gain valuable and profitable market share in an increasingly commoditized telecoms market. Most companies would kill to be in the same position in that industry. But the company had a problem: it did not like to spend capital (Capex) unless it got insane and way over market returns. Sounds good from an economics professor's point of view, but in the real world it caused major problems.

I was asked to create the business case to justify spending over $20 million on a new data center. The center was to house a large number of racks as well as provide the latest and greatest technology so that the company could maintain its leadership in the market. The new center had multiple power and bandwidth feeds, dual fire suppression systems, biometric security scanners, twenty-four-inch thick walls to prevent interference and any storm damage since it was located where hurricanes sometimes hit––in short, it was every IT manager's wet dream. You could not build a better data center with today's technology. We had customers lining up to rent rack space; in fact, it was 35% presold the day it finally opened.

The issue was the return. We originally forecasted that the new data center would pay for itself within three and a half years (i.e., the cash flow from the renting of rack space, capacity, etc., over three and a half years would pay for the entire $20 million initial investment, and after that it would be at least 60% pure profit). We repeatedly forecasted payback would take over three years under multiple scenarios. That was not good enough for management at the firm. We then started to play with the assumptions and got the payback down to two and three-quarters years. In the telecom industry, it never gets better than that on a large capital spend; in fact, most of the returns typically take five to seven years before the investment pays for itself. If I had shown one of the business cases to any of the other companies in the industry, they would have beat me over the head trying to hand me a check to build it, or they would have kicked my ass out of the conference room for wasting their time with pie-in-the-sky numbers. Unfortunately, it was not good enough for this company. They wanted their money back in less than two years! Short of the company dealing with loan-shark type of loans or having drug dealers stashing money in the data center, I did not know how we could get this return. Then, a colleague turned me on to how the board worked with the company.

The board of directors for the company had to approve any business case with a cost over $1 million. They did not like to spend more than 4% of their revenue on capital expenditures (industry average at the time was close to 12%) so that they could enhance their return on equity and presumably get a higher stock price in the short-term. Forget about the fact that over the long run they would look even better with profitable growth; they were only concerned about the next quarter, not three years from now. That was somebody else's issue. I guess this type of thing happens when you get upper management and board turnover constantly. Occasionally, the board would spend above the 4% Capex limit if a business case offered impossible returns.

That is Bizarro world. In the real world, nobody ever went back and checked to see if the actual returns were ever made because most of the management and board was typically replaced before the projects where completed and reviewed. This situation made it ripe for business case infla-tion. If management and the board wanted payback within two years, they got it or you did not get the money for your business case. So, instead of get-ting realistic business cases, employees would juice the numbers to make their returns incredibly high so as to get the money for their pet projects.

Normally, a typical Internal Rate of Return (IRR) would be approximately 20%; this caused the IRR numbers increase to over 60%. We had to forecast that the data center would be sold out within nine months of opening the door, keeping in mind that it took almost four years to fill the last data center that they built. Using this logic, it would have made sense to approve two new data centers to be built since they usually take ten to twelve months to complete.

The business case took an extra nine months to get approved because of the back and forth negotiations to accelerate the payback period. We did over fifteen different iterations of the business case before it was finally approved by the board. The delay also cost the company a lot of money. By the time the business case was approved, the company's last data center had completely sold out. This was a large blow to the company. The data center was one of the star products that lifted top-line revenue as well as increased the bottom-line profit. Sensing that revenue growth was declin-ing, the board panicked; they wanted the new data center fast-tracked and built in less than the original eleven months that was forecasted. Like in auto racing, if you want to go faster, it generally costs more money.

When the design was completed, they put the construction plans out to bid to a handful of companies to hopefully lower the costs of construc-tion. Normally, this is a good practice, but if you demand that something gets built within 75% of the normal time, you generally get three types of responses. The first type you get is from the experienced builders who know that to do it right it takes a certain amount of time. You either have to cut corners, hire more people, or work longer hours. The experienced builders raised their prices, knowing they had to throw more bodies at the build out.

The second type of builder is new to this type of construction and grossly underestimates the costs and time, and typically does not deliver. The third type is very similar to the second type, except they understand the costs and time constraints, but also realize that the tight timelines could put them in the driver seat for overage costs and hold the project hostage with the intention of getting more money at a later date. Notice how all three cost you more in the end. And that is what happened with the construction. Luckily, we put an additional $2 million into the business case for cost overruns. The amount of extra cost was closer to $2.75 million (total around $20.75 million). Instead of potentially coming in under budget, they actually exceeded budget because of the time constraint. Without the constraint, they probably could have built it for around $18 million, and actually gotten a faster payback than the three and a half years originally projected. Instead, they now have a more expensive data center with an impossible payback period. It will be interesting to see how it turns out.

Lesson to Learn From This Chapter

The lesson is not that lower-ranking people are sneaky and will try to do anything to get their projects approved. The lesson is that management had unrealistic expectations and begged the people below them to lie to them. People do what human beings have been doing since the dawn of time. They act like U.S. Marines and adapt to the situation. If management created an environment where people had a clear understanding of where they wanted to take the business, instead of some dollar figure or numbers on the page, the business cases would have been more realistic. The reason they would have been more realistic is they would have known ahead of time that the case would have been approved because the business truly would need to spend the money on a project that would take it in the direction of its goals. Instead, most management today only cares about hitting this quarter's or this year's numbers. The only direction that makes it to the people doing the work is, "We are not making this quarter's revenue or profit number." That is not a way to run a company, at least if you want it to be successful in the long run.

CHAPTER 5

Perpetual Reorg and the Lag Factor

We have all seen it. The way the American businesses have taken to the surefire method of increasing their stock price: reorganizations and layoffs. This is not new, but the zeal that we have seen in the last decade is what makes this phenomenon so shocking. I once read a research report from a stockbroker that did a study and found that companies that announced layoffs had a 5% higher stock price in the following twelve months compared to companies that did not. So, as you guessed it, Wall Street likes a company that is so poorly run that it needs to get rid of some of its employees. All Wall Street sees is the potential for higher earnings in the future.

Granted, Wall Street does have a point, if a company is truly smart and gets rid of its deadwood (i.e., the third of the people who should not even be there). But what Wall Street doesn't get is the scenario that is most likely happening in these businesses. I provide two different points of view.

First, the managers' point of view. Typically, managers see it two ways. If this is the first reorg/layoff in a while, they are a little shocked. They probably have built up bodies to justify their importance over the last few years. That manager is concerned because less people could mean the manager is less valuable in the company's eyes. They panic and swear on a stack of bibles that they cannot lose anybody and everyone is pulling their weight (even though they know that this not entirely true). Over the next few weeks, reality sinks in and they start offering up some of the least productive members of their team to be on the layoff list.

This is typically what Wall Street rewards. The investors realize that after a while an organization collects deadwood like a person accumulates old stuff in a basement or garage. Every so often you need to do a little spring cleaning.

In some organizations, reorganizations, or "reorgs," and layoffs happen like clockwork. They usually happen about two months prior to the end of the fiscal year. This is designed to give managers and HR enough time to fire these people (excuse me, eliminate their positions) before the reorg messes up the next fiscal year. Heaven forbid redundancy charges screw up the first quarter of the new fiscal year.

Typically, managers in this type of organization know the routine. Instead of spending any effort in firing the people that suck (typically, it can take up to nine months in most states with the amount of documentation that is needed), they just wait until four months prior to the end of the fiscal year to start making a list. They make a slacker list (my words, but you get the drift) by polling their direct reports to see who is not pulling their weight in the organization. In turn, these direct reports are supposed to get rid of any problem employees or anybody else who pissed them off this morning on the way to the coffee machine.

The problems with this type of layoff are twofold. One, the whole basis for this is that the upper management probably does not have a clue how to run the business. Management that tends to do these once-a-year layoffs also tends to be focused on short-term numbers and not focused on taking a company in a long-term direction. Wall Street might tell you that this is the way to do it, but in reality, it is akin to driving a supertanker and focusing on the next one hundred feet in front of you while ignoring the rocks a quarter mile ahead. A supertanker can take up to two miles to stop or change direction. It is this type of short-term thinking that leads to long-term headaches.

Look at successful companies that think long-term, like Apple and Google. When was the last time you heard of any of these companies doing layoffs?

The second reason this type of reorg is bad is because of the employees, or to be specific, the third of the employees who do 90% of the work. Since they are superstars, they are usually told about the reorg ahead of time by their line managers.

Scenarios like this play out all the time. The star employee goes home that night and tells his or her significant other or best friend about the pending layoffs. That person usually replies, "You work your ass off and there might be a chance that you are laid off, too. What about little Bobby's college fund, this house, or the car payment? What are you going to do?" That gets the star nervous. He or she can't sleep. He or she feels like shit for days. Word gets around to his or her friends and colleagues that have gone to other companies. He or she gets the call.

"I heard there might be layoffs at XYZ corp. Are you affected?" asks his or her old boss, who has moved on to greener pastures.

The star replies, "I do think I'm affected, but I won't know until they announce it next Tuesday." The former boss says, "Why don't you meet me for lunch to have a quick talk about you working for me again?" The former boss knows this person works his or her ass off. It would make the boss's job easier to have a star working for him or her again, knowing the star's work ethic. The star goes to the lunch and is rewarded with an extra $10K in annual salary for jumping to a different company.

At the same time, word gets out among the masses that there is going to be a layoff in the next couple of weeks. All work comes to a screeching halt. The productive workers panic (one-third that actually do the work) and start spending every free minute gossiping about what is happening and who is going to be fired. This is when the slackers step up. They realize their days are numbered. They start working like they have never worked before, or at least since the last reorg. They hope they can stem the forces of the reorg long enough that they can stay another year with the company.

So instead of XYZ corp. getting rid of a few slackers, a couple of stars leave ahead of the reorg. This causes the managers to panic at XYZ corp. Instead of getting rid of the slackers, a couple are promoted (maybe even some of the ones who are now diligently doing their jobs, finally) to fill the hole left from the star leaving. The managers do this because they now have one less in the headcount that they need to get rid of, and they know they cannot hire anyone to fill the star's role for at least sixty days after the reorg. They need bodies. They keep the least offending slacker of the group, with a little bit of skills to partially fill the role left vacant by the star leaving.

In this situation, XYZ corporation is clearly worse off. Instead of cleaning house, they got rid of a few stars and only the worst of the slackers. Still, some slackers remain, and now they are "trying" to fill the role left vacant by the stars. Remember, the stars are the ones doing most of the work. So if you lose some stars, it means more work now falls on fewer people, so unless someone steps up in the slacker world, the managers have more work to do. This, in itself, is a problem. The stars that remain quickly get overworked and start looking to leave. So instead of the cream rising to the top, we find out crap really does float.

Perpetual Reorg

I once worked for a company that had so many reorgs that no sooner than they would finish one, another reorg would start. What started this was the company decided to buy parts of the number two player in the industry, which was being broken apart by the purchase of the number one player due to regulatory reasons. In the late 1990s, a conglomerate that owned the second largest company in a certain Internet segment had the chance to buy out the largest company in that segment. The largest company in that segment was seen as the crown jewel of Internet. The only way the conglomerate would be allowed to purchase the number one player was to sell parts of its current business or spin off the company it owned. If the conglomerate was able to keep both companies, it would have dominant control (i.e., over 50% market share in one of the fastest-growing markets that the U.S. government was trying to nurture). In other words, the government would not allow the purchase. The only way the conglomerate could buy the number one player would be to sell off most of the number two player that it owned.

The company I worked for had visions of leap-frogging from the number six position to being the number two player in the U.S. They approached the conglomerate and struck a deal with them to purchase the number two player. When they made this purchase, it changed the entire company. The business transformed from a decently run business to one where management determined they could spend like mad because they were now big shots in the industry. They were the new number two player, and suddenly Wall Street and everyone in the industry knew who they were.

After they made the purchase, the revenue and profit numbers immediately went to crap. It seems like the number one player in the industry was smart enough to make sure that all the decent employees from the old number two player were moved to the number one player. The conglomerate was smart. It knew that when it purchased the number one player, there would be a lot of overlap in positions. It decided, long before being ordered by the Federal Trade Commission (FTC) to break apart the company, that it needed to reduce headcount. Now that it had this order, it went through and made sure that the people it kept were the one-third that actually did most of the work. It loaded the carcass of (what was left after they got a couple of crown jewels) the number two player it was selling to the number six player with every new fresh-out-of-college kid or long-term worthless soul it could so that it did not have to pay severance packages to the people it was already planning on firing.

The conglomerate received at least half the cost of the purchase of the number one player back within thirty days of the purchase by spinning off the unwanted pieces to the smaller player. It also stuck the smaller player with the costs of having to pay future severance packages for the people the conglomerate was already planning on firing in a reorg. The smaller player, at first, provided bonuses to retain these new people because it felt that they must be the experts because they were the number two player and the purchaser was only the number six player. In addition, a lot of the number two player salaries were a lot higher than the number six player salaries. The existing employees at the number six player bitched and moaned until they got increased salaries and perks to match what the people at the number two player were earning. Consultants feasted on large consulting contracts by helping management with ideas on how to integrate the two companies. Everyone was making money except the company.

This process of integration took at least six months. Costs skyrocketed. Nobody paid attention to new sales. Business plummeted as existing customers of the number two player left for more competent companies. The board freaked out, rightly so. They in turn brought in more new management consultants. The consultants quietly suggested to the board that they should replace the CEO. They agreed. The CEO and most of the upper management were removed in a clean sweep.

Since the numbers did not improve within the eight to nine months after the reorg, the board got antsy. They wondered if they hired the wrong person. So they started putting the new CEO on an even tighter leash. They asked the new CEO about why the costs were high in relation to revenue (obviously this was a direct factor of them no longer growing and the number of employees staying the same or slightly increasing). Then the board would bring in the new management consultants (every time). The consultants looked at the revenue-to-cost figures and agreed there needed to be a new round of layoffs because the business was not meeting the average ratios of other companies in their industry. CEO 101 would start all over again.

The board now demanded that the new CEO do another round of layoffs. All that the new round of layoffs did was cause more delays to returning to growth. Fearing the worst, the board decided to start quietly interviewing possible CEO replacements for the company. The new management consultants also screened potential candidates, by the way, as another of their services they conveniently offer. So the search for the new CEO happened again and again.

The board kept changing management every nine months or so. The company had seven CEOs in less than five years. (I am sorry, but seven? Where was the board of directors? They should be fired and replaced, too. This clearly shows incompetence knows no bounds.) Every time you got a new CEO, you got a new vision. They would do all the tricks they teach you in CEO 101. The problem was short-term tricks were not what was needed. Long-term stable thinking, a solid vision, and sticking to the basics were sorely needed.

The only thing that all this change was doing was putting this company in a constant state of shellshock. Nothing got done at all for the four months surrounding a reorg. Employees and managers were scared or too lost to make any effective changes. All this did was seal the fate of any new CEOs. They could not execute their "vision" in the nine months after the reorg. There was simply not enough time.

This went on like this for about four and a half years before the company finally went bankrupt. They claimed it was because of a failed purchase of a competitor's business, but the truth is that the board failed. They had grandiose ideas and Wall Street's funny money but no common sense. Plus they did not understand the *lag factor*.

Lag Factor

The lag factor is simple to understand but hard to counter In real life. The lag factor is the delay in time between when an initial action is taken before the desired (or undesired) result or change takes place. Sometimes this is called percussion and repercussion. The lag factor is directly related to two things: size of the organization and the length it has been in business. It is a lot harder to get a change implemented and followed across an organization the size of GM versus Bob's Plumbing down the street. GM has (or should I say, had) hundreds of thousands of employees. Bob's Plumbing might have six. Also working against GM is how long it has been in business and, more importantly, how set in their ways management and employees are. GM has unions, and traditionally unions have been set in their ways and resistant to change mainly because they feel that management is out to get them. You know what they say: "You might be paranoid, but it doesn't mean that somebody isn't out there trying to get you."

The lag factor is important for management to understand. If management does not understand this, they will continuously try to make changes, thinking things are not working, when in fact they are, but there is simply just a delay in getting the change implemented. The more management tries to make changes, the more it screws up the company and sends mixed messages to their employees, and the less work that actually gets done.

It is also important for Wall Street to understand. Wall Street has an extremely bad habit of wanting rapid changes and interfering with companies it feels are not making the changes fast enough. If Wall Street stopped smoking pixie dust in the rarified air up in the ivory towers and actually learned how to run a business, they would learn that 99% of a business cannot change on the dime. They could actually make more money by finding CEOs who are long-term-focused with a vision and the patience to obtain it over time. Well-run companies have a true economic advantage that is not easily overcome by the hordes of imitators.

Typically, a true vision change takes anywhere from eight to forty-eight months to completely take place, depending on how entrenched the company is to start with (either with employee size or length of time it has been in business). First, the CEO or upper management needs to come up with a long-term strategy. This can take anywhere from five minutes to a lifetime for some. I think you should give it one to two months. The next step is in communicating the changes. This can take anywhere from one to six months, depending how widespread the company is or how sweeping the changes are. Now we are up to eight months and counting. Next comes the implementation phase. The implementation phase is the longest because you usually encounter past cultural behaviors and entrenched people who already have a lot invested in the current system. This phase can take anywhere from six months to three or more years. So if my math is correct (remember, I did go to public schools in the hippie days of the '70s and '80s; needless to say, I can't spell or do math in my head), you are looking at a minimum time of eight months up to almost four years.

The sad thing is, American business thinks this is too long. What boards of Directors and Wall Street miss is that it is a lot faster to hire good management with a vision and tenacity to succeed than to keep rehiring CEOs and implementing their visions for nine months and repeating the process. Every time an organization goes through the process, the slower the actual results are. In short, what most of the boards of directors and Wall Street are doing is ruining the very companies they are trying to invest in for the long-term.

The Never-Ending Reorg

This is the worst reorg story that I have. I once worked for a company that had been doing regular reorgs every eighteen to twenty-four months. The company was a large telecom company that went from conducting business in a monopoly market to a fully deregulated market. It had too many people and had to thin down as competition ate into its market share and profits. This is totally understandable. It sucked for the workers who did not get laid off. The ones that got laid off got large checks worth four to six weeks' pay for every year they worked. Some had worked twenty to thirty years. This did not even include the pension top-ups. These sorts of severance packages would make an automaker union employee jealous.

This telecom company would also deploy other techniques to "maximize shareholder value." The board also became big fans of "sweating assets," i.e., keeping antiquated shit running for one more year using bubble gum and duct tape instead of investing in better technologies and equipment, just to save a few bucks. They repeatedly only invested 4% to 6% of revenue in capital projects, and then only in must-haves and big pet projects.

Typically, telecom companies spend 10% to 15% per year in capital projects because of the nature of the industry. This company is still using databases that were built in 1997 for Windows 95/XP that have not been supported by the manufacturer since 2000 (I am writing this in 2010; and they do not even work with Windows 7 operating systems). The company is on version four of a popular data-reporting software package, when the database manufacturer is currently on version thirteen and had stopped supporting version ten because it was deemed too old.

After five to six years of doing this, and four CEOs later, the board decided to bring in a CEO from one of its sister companies based in the UK. This CEO was a fan of American-style reorgs. So the first thing he did was bring in a management consulting company to tell the company that, according to industry statistics, a company with $XXX million in revenue should only be supported by Y thousands of employees. So according to the CEO, this was an opportunity to eliminate a further 30% to 40% of the employees so that the company can say it is running it like a typical telecom company. Management and the consultants did not care that the company did not have efficient systems to allow the employees to work like better run companies in their industry. They knew that in two years (or less), management would get a large payout and not have to deal with the repercussions. That was somebody else's issue.

The challenge with this approach was that the statistics for the industry assume that the company operates with a basic level of efficiency and is not kept together with duct tape. To get rid of 30% to 40% of your people is a large task. Basically, the process is done with a shotgun. You need bodies and lots of them to fill the quota. You do not care who; it just has to be somebody, and the more expensive their salary, the better. In most companies (even poorly run ones), a large part of the third that does all the work tends to get the higher salaries so as to keeping the working fools from becoming restless and leaving. During this reorg, management decided to combine multiple branches of the company into just one branch so they could run it more efficiently, regardless of any geographic differences.

This set the stage for the classic reorg-and-layoff issue. The good people tend to get the word earlier. They also know that more than likely they will land on their feet because work still needs to get done. Sprinkle in four to six weeks of pay for every year of work, plus a top-up in pension amounts so that the employee can have a fully funded retirement account. Couple that with the knowledge that whoever is left will have a crap load of work to do in keeping the sinking ship afloat. Top it up with the fact that the people who were making the decisions about who stayed or left were consultants from a different country with a job to do in a short period of time, and what do you get? You get an extremely expensive run for the door by the people who were keeping the lights on.

Within the first six weeks, 10% of the employees left, most volunteering for early retirement or a buyout (majority of the employees that left were the best and brightest, i.e., in the third who do the most work). They had paid out something like $25 to $50 million, almost 10% of their annual revenue, in six weeks. The board freaked out. They had to run to their parent company to ask for more money. The reorg stopped dead in its tracks, or so it seemed.

Instead of stopping the exodus of quality people, people panicked and started leaving without a package because they wanted to leave on their own terms and not wait for some fresh-out-of-business-school twenty-something "expert" to fire them. More of the people who had been there awhile took early retirement since their union and management contracts allowed it once they met the minimum service lengths, thus adding to the cash drain. They quickly found other jobs in the industry. In fact, other companies in the industry took to poaching the quality people. The other companies saw the potential to get quality people at a fraction of the cost since most wanted to keep working and were now receiving their pensions. It always amazed me that neither their contracts nor their exit documents forbade them from working for the competition for any set period of time after they left.

After another couple of months, the company doing the reorg saw that barely any work was getting done and revenue was on a steady decline. Funny how that happened, eh? To stop further declines, the company started trying to rush the reorg and make positions for the quality people and provide them with retention bonuses. Yeah, that's right, what started as a round of massive layoffs had to be slowed and retention bonuses issued for some key positions.

Jump forward six months into a totally screwed-up reorg. The company promised investors cost savings. They needed to make the best of a screwed-up year. They restarted the reorg. This time, they came up with an even more brilliant idea: have everyone interview for their current jobs. As part of this reorg, they were trying to combine functions using the wonderful Matrix Management system that I spoke so *highly* of before, across thirteen different countries. They would still operate in the multiple countries but a lot of the back-office departments like finance, marketing, and network management, would be combined to generate "efficiencies." When combining multiple locations into one virtual location, the theory is that if you have ten locations with ten people performing the same role and you combine the jobs, you would only need maybe two or three people and can eliminate the other seven. This is sound in theory because maybe the two or three people getting the new position would be your third of the overachievers. In practice, this is extremely hard to pull off without proper training and advanced systems, which the company did not provide. This company went one step further. They brought in ten HR consultants who were mandated to attend all interviews, and their input had to be weighed in the choosing process on who got the job and who didn't. Typically, in this type of situation, the direct line manager knows who does his or her job well and who should find another line of business. Not using this direct information and having to wait to get the ten HR "experts" to determine who should get the job was a total time-waster. It was impossible to schedule any interviews because they had to now get three people (HR "expert," line manager or hiring manager, and the employee; two of whom had extremely tight schedules) to agree to a time when all three could meet for the interview.

In business as in college, theories are best left on whiteboards. In the real world, here is what happens. If the role is one of power (i.e., higher up) you typically have five to seven people who are in the third who do the job effectively. They do one of three things when they find out they need to interview again for their job. First, they start cozying up to the decision maker or their new potential boss as a way to position themselves for a future role. Truly the ass-kissers' move of a decade if there was one. If they get their jobs this way, they have sold their souls and are now somebody's bitch. The second thing that happens is if they have to interview again, they decide, "What the hell, if I have to do it once, why not with another company?" This is where the best usually go unless they get the quiet tap on the shoulder from management telling them they have the job already. The third thing they do is retire or start their own businesses. Rarely do the quality, hardworking people wait around to be picked if they are already in management. They know they have a skill that is of use, and they plan to use it.

So now we are seven months into a reorg, and finally the upper management (top two layers) have been assigned. The third layer is now busy getting their teams together. Normally in this situation, we are usually only two to three weeks into a reorg, not seven months. So, basically, nobody has been watching the business for seven months, and it has gone completely down the crapper. Instead of growing 5% per year, the business was off up to 10% in some markets. The top layer of management started to get scared. They saw the gleam in the boards members' eyes that they were getting antsy to call in more management consultants and fire them. The CEO leaned heavily on his direct reports to produce something and start to turn things around. Unfortunately, the second and third layers of management had not put together their teams yet because they needed to finish interviewing the people who actually do the physical work. The more you go down the layers of management, the greater the number of people there is on each layer. So the third layer was now trying to do everything: interview for their new teams, do the work that their nonexistent teams were supposed to be doing, and perform for their new bosses. This was burn-out city. A lot of the third layer decided that sucked and left the company, thus causing more people to have to be interviewed.

Months eight, nine, ten, and eleven of the reorg looked like this. Some of the third layer did ten-minute crap interviews just to get bodies to fill the roles that they had. They really did not listen in the interviews even though they had the "help" of the "expert" HR staff who had to be at every interview (the HR consultants tried to make it a longer process, but practicality worked out). Also during this time were the holidays where people often took extended time off. This did not help with expediting the process one bit. Also, during one of the months, a ruling came down from upper management that said the company would no longer hire consultants to do any of the job roles. Employees had to be full-time. This led to more openings that had to have replacement workers, requiring even more interviews and distracting people from actually getting any work done.

The fourth and fifth layers got filled by the twelfth month. This was fine for some because they had jobs. Others left the company one way or another (a fair chunk did not make it through the process, which was the intended result). The ones with the jobs started to get nervous. A rumor quickly made its rounds. The third layer had finally started getting their offer letters from HR, and a lot of them received pay cuts or benefit decreases or both. Remember, the company was trying to save money. People in the fourth and fifth layers started fearing the worst and started trying to get their package details. This put massive pressure on the ten HR experts to produce offer letters for over seven hundred people in a short span of time. This resulted in errors, usually not in favor of the employee, on the offer letters. Between the rumors and the error-laden offer letters, people started quitting and going to other companies and the competition. Thus, another round of interviews for replacements started.

In this new round of change in months thirteen and fourteen, the company had to try to call back people they had either let go or who had left on their own terms, or try to keep some of the consultants who were slated to leave (a lot of the consultants had also started looking for new consulting contracts and started to leave on their own). Failing that, they had to start from scratch and bring in people from the outside or bring in people who were not really up to the competency level to fill the vacancies.

By the fifteenth month, everything was settled. The company was leaner by four hundred plus people in the back offices: marketing, finance, etc. There were no more consultants, or dramatically fewer. I was one of the consultants to turn down an offer to be an employee because they simply offered less than what I was making working for other companies. The company's operating costs looked better on a go-forward basis. The only problem was that revenue numbers were still in the toilet. This was to be expected given that for fifteen months, little or no new activities were done to help increase market share, enter new markets, or create new products. Now that the teams were in place, they had to perform. So everybody tried to cram in fifteen months of work into sixty days with a staff that was smaller and just learning their new roles and processes. Talk about some major bottlenecks. In some key financial, marketing, and system development roles, there were clearly not enough people for the normal times not to mention the new cram-everything-out-in-sixty-days environment. The business was paralyzed. It now took three to four times longer to perform the same functions compared to before the reorg.

I left the company around this timeframe. The last I heard, the board was starting to look for a new CEO and management team to try to "fix" the broken business. If the board would just let the new teams perform before trying to do another change, they might make it. If not, this company is in a death spiral.

Lesson to Learn From This Chapter

The lesson to learn from this chapter is simple: constant reorgs and reorgs that never end destroy a company from within. Sometimes reorgs are really needed. They are needed for failing companies or companies that need to change direction because the industry is changing or where they want the business to go is changing. I am in 100% agreement with doing those reorgs. It is the companies that do them every twelve to eighteen months that are abusing themselves. The good employees leave because they do not want to work for companies that are so poorly run that they need to always be changing direction. The remaining employees are either extremely overworked if they are competent or extremely out of their fields if they are average or poor performers. Some would argue that reorgs cause the average worker to rise to the occasion. This does happen for some, but most just bitch and moan and hold the organization back. After enough reorgs, an organization gets a stink around it that drives the good away and attracts the poor performers, thus causing more and more reorgs in the future.

CHAPTER 6

The Presentation From Hell (How to Make Enemies and Disillusion Staff All in the Same Half Hour)

I once worked for a company that was a monopoly provider of telecom services in a large country in the Caribbean. It was a small division of a large global telecom provider. They were extremely profitable because the government encouraged them to keep the prices high so that they could receive a large check annually from the company as a "licensing fee," or tax. This licensing fee funded some of the governmental expenditures and thus helped the government keep taxes for employees extremely low. This resulted in extremely expensive telecom services. Imagine spending $1.25 per minute to make a telephone call to countries like the U.S., Canada, and the UK. Every time there was an election, the politicians would threaten to end the monopoly to play into people's distaste of paying such high telecom fees. Normally the politicians would rethink this after the election because they would have to find a new source of revenue to fund the government if the monopoly was broken.

This went on for years, but eventually people had enough. In the late '90s, the government finally listened and opened up the local telecom market on the island. The opening of the market caused prices to decline by over 90% within ten years. It also cost my client a loss in market share of approximately 50%. They went from a $200-million-a-year business down to a $60-million-a-year business within seven years. They had over four hundred employees before deregulation, dropping to a low of sixty within nine years of deregulation. Before deregulation, over 90% of their revenue was from phone calls, and the rest was from some really old data products that few companies use today. The company needed to change and change quickly, or it would have been bankrupt within a couple of years.

Though it looked bad, the company fought back. They slashed prices repeatedly to fight off the unrelenting competition from the new entrants in the market. They introduced new services like Internet (remember, this was the late '90s) and data centers. They cut costs to the bone. They eliminated almost 85% of the staff within a nine-year period. They outsourced a lot of key roles in an effort to gain efficiencies. They invested in new undersea cable systems to transport data, Internet, and phone calls at a drastically cheaper price. They added new networking systems to further reduce their costs while being able to offer newer and faster products. They revamped their sales team to bring in a new sales force with a proven track record. They added an updated data center to attract new clients. They entered new markets where they could upsell customers complete solutions and not just pieces of a solution where the customer was left to make the pieces work together. In short, the management did what every textbook *Harvard Business Case Review* suggested they do. And it worked.

Starting the eighth year after deregulation, new orders for services like Internet, data circuits, and data centers started offsetting the declining revenue in legacy businesses; in other words, they started to grow again. At first, it was only a handful of percentage points. A promising start to a turnaround but not really mouthwatering results when compared to the new entrants that were still growing at double-digit rates. Management reduced headcount again in an effort to boost profits. It was arguable if this was really needed since most of the fat had already been reduced in the company. It worked in increasing profits, but the management started to get a really bad rap with the employees, many of whom had been there over twenty years and had lived through the dramatic changes in the company. The employees felt that the cuts should have been completed before this round of layoffs since they were seeing a bottoming-out phase in their revenue and market share losses. A large portion of the employees were already working long hours just to do the everyday jobs that were now increasingly concentrated on fewer and fewer individuals. There were employees who were carrying the workload of what four people did prior to the cutbacks. Many were burning out and refusing to do more, but the cuts did not stop. Management was getting addicted to them, thinking, like a long-term junkie, that they could quit whenever they wanted to.

The increased profits and revenue made management look like superstars to their bosses in the global offices. They had turned around a failing business. They had made it almost as profitable, on a percentage basis, as it was prior to deregulation. The global company became addicted to the growth and profitability. They craved more and more. They pushed the division to do more and more cuts in headcount to increase profits even more. At the same time, management would only support capital projects (i.e., projects that were large in nature and usually required multiple years to get a payback) that grew the revenue of the company. They did not want to invest in automating any systems to streamline processes. The employees who were doing the work of four people were expected to keep doing the work of four people, without any updates in tools since the late '90s, even though newer tools would have made them more efficient and presumably made their jobs easier.

The union that supported the lower-level employees was getting tired of having to always sustain cuts after cuts while making the remaining employees work more and more for very minor cost-of-living adjustments. The union pushed back on any changes that were proposed. The union employees and management were always fighting. Both parties continuously made off-the-cuff remarks that amounted to a war of words. I felt that at any time, I could expect a strike to be called.

The next couple of years saw annual increases in revenue and profits in the 8% to 12% range per annum. Headcount was further reduced to forty-five through a mixture of attrition, retirement, and layoffs. Most importantly, the company was able to grow while the new entrants were either not growing or were shrinking during the same period. That clearly showed the company had truly turned the corner—or had it?

The CEO who had managed the transition from monopoly to fully deregulated market got promoted to the next layer of management, where he was put in charge of multiple divisions, including the one where he was CEO previously. He was given this task because the other divisions were losing market share, profitability, and, in some cases, revenue to the competition. He was seen as the savior to the other failing businesses in the group since he had so much experience turning around the failing division in the Caribbean.

During the next twelve months, a new CEO was brought in to grow the original division. The local management and employees felt that finally someone with a management style that included more than cutting costs would step in and make things better. The new CEO definitely had a different style and was looking to shake things up for the better. He was looking at adding new people to the business to help improve some of the areas that had become weaknesses and subsequently would impact any growth plans. The new CEO started the process of getting some of the systems and processes updated to current technologies.

The former CEO could not leave things alone. His management style was clear: he managed by cost cuts. He looked at the other divisions that were now his direct reports. He saw an opportunity to make cuts in all the businesses. He first started making cuts in the operations of the five new divisions that reported to him. He reduced headcount by 15% right off the bat. He reduced capital expenditure from 12% of revenue to 5% of revenue. He reduced marketing expenses from 4% of revenue down to less than 1%. He also started looking at ways he could have the divisions combine resources so that common resources were shared (i.e., by deploying the piss-poor Matrix Management system). Sort of like George W. Bush with tax cuts, this CEO never saw a headcount reduction he did not like. The replacement CEO did not see the change coming until the presentation hit.

The Presentation to All Staff

Twice a year the staff had a mandatory all-hands meeting, where management would show some graphs about revenue and the CFO would talk about needing to control costs. Even though the news was not that bad since they were growing again, management portrayed the numbers in a dark light because they felt people would watch the costs better. Usually the meeting lasted about a half hour, max. Nobody really paid attention typically because they all felt it was great to see the company grow but they were resentful that they did not receive any of the rewards. All the employees ever saw was a measly annual cost-of-living adjustment and more and more work using less and less people with tools that were designed by programmers who had since retired. You could almost view it as the employees being handed gruel and having to thank the management for being fed.

One particular presentation really stands out. The former CEO of the division, now the regional CEO, brought some of his bosses with him to present the new structure across all the divisions he controlled. The first few slides were the traditional financial number slides that people seem to ignore. The next couple of slides woke up the catatonic crowd. They presented the new management structure across the divisions. The new structure was based on Matrix Management (vomit), which never seems to work. At first, everybody thought this was nice to know until they recognized that every single person who reported to the top level was not from the division that had just turned itself around. The new divisional CEO was nowhere to be found on the slides. None of the head people from the division in marketing, networks, finance, etc. were in charge. Everybody that was in power and had experience turning around a declining business now reported up through people who had no experience even though their divisions needed to be reorganized. Instead of making the division with the experience the center of excellence within the company, the regional CEO treated that division like lepers to be shunned. The new CEO of the resurrected division became a title head who just met with local governmental figures but had very little control over the people who were under him since they technically reported to other groups (God, do I love Matrix Management). The new CEO was pissed. He took the job because he was extremely qualified, but now he looked like a highly paid babysitter.

To top that off, the regional CEO went through five more slides showing employees that some of their jobs were no longer needed and their roles would be moved to other parts of the company or to offshore companies to save money. Unfortunately, the people who were losing their jobs found out in front of everybody. There were people crying during this meeting. Before this meeting, the dynamics of the corporation set the union versus the management. The minute the regional CEO presented this, the dynamics changed to be the employees (all of them, including the union AND management) versus the regional CEO. It was the quickest employee mood change I have ever seen.

People stood there in shock. They could not believe their eyes. They thought they had already been through the apocalypse with resurrecting the company from a fallen angel to a superstar. They were expecting to be rewarded for their efforts. They at least expected to be seen as experts to help the other divisions or, at a minimum, to receive a pat on the back. Instead, they got kicked in the teeth at the goal line by their own player.

The regional CEO finished the presentation and asked if there were any questions. Normally, the Q&A session would take five, ten minutes, tops. People typically asked stupid questions to make themselves look good. That did not happen here. There was a flurry of questions. Literally 50% of the staff had their hands up. People were pissed. They asked a lot of hard questions the CEO tried to expertly deflect. Nobody was having it. They did not let him off the hook. It got so bad that the regional CEO's boss had to jump in to save him. The Q&A session went on for over one hour more, even after the regional CEO's boss tried to take over the meeting. Many people stayed late just to ask tough questions. I stood there personally wanting to ask some questions but kept my mouth shut. I was a long-term consultant and not an employee. Even though I felt I should say something, it was not my place and the employees did not appear to need my help.

Normally, I am one of the first people to support capitalism, but this is where greed actually harms capitalism. Upper management was getting too greedy. They wanted performance regardless of the people they burned to get it. Here were the people who had done the impossible. They helped save a dying business by being extremely frugal. They had seen literally hundreds of their friends and colleagues laid off. They had spent long hours doing more and more work while watching other people in the same industry get paid more. These weren't some workers working in a dying industry where the company itself was failing. These were people who worked for a growing company that had profit margins greater than 40%. They were the envy of the local telecom industry, and the company acted like it was going to file bankruptcy any day.

Lesson to Learn From This Chapter

This lesson is one of tact. Do not abuse the people who have taken you from an impossible situation and turned it around and made you look good. This presentation reminded me of the scene in *The Simpson Movie* where Homer was trying to get back to Springfield after being trapped in Alaska. His only mode of transportation was a dogsled. To keep the dogs going, he used a bullwhip and cracked it on the dogs. He would crack the whip to have them do everything, like go forward, jump a cavern, and go to sleep. The minute he untied the dogs to allow them to eat, the dogs turned on him and started mauling him. In this presentation, the staff, union, **and** management turned on the regional CEO and started attacking him in front of his boss. The regional CEO would not quit "beating" the employees, and they turned on him like a cornered dog that has been beaten too much. It was not a pretty sight. If you take care of the people who take care of your company, they will take care of you. They will surprise you with what they can do. Transversely, if you abuse them, they will eventually do the same to you.

CHAPTER 7

Redundancy by Shooting Yourself in the Foot

Ah, layoffs! What is a business book without a quick discussion about layoffs? It seems like everywhere you look today, there is nothing but layoffs. Instead of calling them the American term "layoff," I kind of prefer the British term "redundancy." Redundancy has a slightly more eloquent ring to it. Making someone redundant implies that you do not have any work for their position, so you need to eliminate it. It's the workload not **you**. The American term layoff sounds like you are dumping your problems on society, which you really are, kind of. Who do you think pays for the unemployment wages? Society does. To me, this sounds a lot more negative. Instead of losing the job because the business does not have work for you, you are being laid off on society like a castaway or a common hobo, to quote my ten-year-old.

However you phrase it, a redundancy can be done the right way or the wrong way. The right way usually involves giving the employees either adequate notice, usually sixty to ninety days, that their jobs are being made redundant or providing a few months' severance package to make sure the employees can survive the period between jobs. Unfortunately, as shown in the Perpetual Reorg and the Lag Factor chapter, this does not usually happen so graciously. Redundancies also sometimes hit the absolutely wrong person at the wrong time and can be detrimental to the company. Nobody is irreplaceable, but some are very close. Here is a story that shows the point. Timing is everything.

Making the Head of the Union Job Redundant

I once worked for a telecom company that had an absolutely terrible relationship with its unionized employees. The company viewed these employees as lazy, unproductive, overpaid babies always crying about this thing or that. The employees had extreme mistrust with management. More than once, they were promised that there would not be any redundancies, only to find a new round thirty to sixty days later. The employees viewed the management as greedy lying people that you couldn't turn your back on without being stabbed from behind. The truth was somewhere in the middle. Both sides had built up their biases over many years. It was almost like the McCoys' and Hatfields' feuding. Neither side remembers what started the animosity but both remember the last thing that was done to them. It almost got comical when both sides would go out of the way to screw the other side.

To make matters worse, the company also had a philosophy of always shrinking their labor force. They reduced their employees almost 50% in the couple years that I did business with them. The rub for the employees was that the company was still solidly profitable and that most of the cuts were not necessary. They were done just to fatten the bottom line without any concern about long-term sustainability of the company, just to enrich the management with ever-larger bonuses. This led to the union asking for large wage adjustments every couple of years when their contract expired. They felt like their workers were having to work harder because there were less people and more work to be done. The employees also felt that the management bonuses were based on their hard work. They felt that they did not receive any of the upside but had almost all of the downside.

This went on year after year. The union asked for larger-than-inflation increases in salary. Management tried to plead poverty or a tough business environment to get the increases to match or improve on inflation, just to lower their cost of personnel on an income statement.

In late 2007, the company promoted a new VP of human resources (HR), a lady who was in management for a number of years. The company had invested literally over $100K in helping her get her PhD in psychology to help her career in the HR field. The company had a rule where it required an employee to have to work for the company for two years after completing a degree at the company's expense, in addition to working while seeking the degree. The VP of HR did not mind the additional years of work that were required for the company to pay for her degree because she felt that she was expanding her worth to a company by getting her PhD.

To show how valuable she had become to the organization, it decided to have her take the lead in negotiating the annual pay increases with the union. In the past, she had been part of the team led by the CEO during the union negotiations. During the negotiations, the company was also in the process of merging with another division of the larger parent company. The other division had a full range of employees and was looking to cut more staff.

The union was experiencing turnover at the management level. They had been training one of the company's employees to take a bigger and bigger role within the union. She had a long positive history with the company and the union. She was always responsive and tried to bring the two sides together instead of ranting about the past history of poor relations. The union flew her to different events around the U.S. so that she could learn negotiation and management skills. She also had a decent relationship with the VP of HR. They were not friends, but they did sometimes frequent the same places and chitchatted together regularly at work.

In early 2008, they had to renegotiate a contract for the employees covered under the union contract. The union wanted a 5% rate increase in salary even though the inflation rate was less than 3%. Management only wanted to increase the union wages by 2.5%. Management also wanted to expand a lot of roles currently done by the union employees to allow them to handle more tasks in their job descriptions. They wanted this so that they could merge the two divisions and cut heads and still get the jobs that needed to get done, done. The union was against this because they were more interested in protecting current jobs and did not want to see any more redundancies.

Negotiation got off to a good start. Both sides presented their positions. There was a feeling that they could bridge the gap in the wage increase. They had regular weekly meetings, and negotiations were cordial. It seemed that both sides were working through their issues, and an agreement appeared eminent. Unfortunately, the division merger happened and the negotiations went to hell very quickly.

The first thing that happened in the division merger was the rumors of redundancies. Employees and management heard rumors that a lot of the different functionalities (both union and non-union) would be consolidated into the other division. The rumors caused the negotiation with the union to stall out.

During the delay in negotiations, some of the management changes took place. The rumors proved true, and management announced a 10% reduction in employees across the two combined divisions. The VP of HR was told that they decided to go with the VP of HR from the other division and that her role would be terminated within ninety days, but she was still expected to finish negotiating the union contract. The VP of HR was ecstatic about losing her job. Apparently, she had wanted to leave to get more money from other companies that would reward her for having her PhD. The only thing holding her back was the thought of having to pay back the company the almost $100K in tuition costs if she left before the two years were up.

The president of the union found out her role was made redundant and that she had to find another role within the merged divisions within ninety days. Like her counterpart, she was told to finish negotiating the contract before her job disappeared. She was shocked. She was always a high achiever who seemed to step up to help everyone. Most people would never have guessed that she was in a union or guessed that she was the president of the union because of her positive attitude versus the negative stigma in society that union employees tend to have.

The two groups met again to try to hammer out the agreement before the ninety-day deadline. The meetings took a predicable turn for the worse. The VP of HR was not really concerned about the outcome of the negotiations. She was more concerned about finding a new, higher-paying job now that she had her PhD. The president of the union was pissed off that she had to apply for a new job within the company or she would be made redundant. To recap, the management representative really did not care about the how the negotiation panned out; all she cared about was finishing them. The union representative was upset about the planned 10% labor reduction, potentially including her. So we now had one person just wanting to do whatever it took to finish negotiating and one person who was so pissed off that she was not willing to give an inch. Guess what side had better results negotiating? You guessed it, the union. They wound up getting almost a 4% wage increase and only had to give up slightly on the flexibility of different roles.

Lesson to Learn From This Chapter

The lesson from this chapter is one of timing. There is a right time and a wrong time for everything. Clearly, this company had the wrong timing and it cost them in the end. This is almost like trying to tell your wife that she might want to lose some weight on your anniversary night. If you do that, you will remember that anniversary night for all the wrong reasons.

You will remember it for that one large fight and not for the rekindling of your romance. It boils down to patience. If the company had waited to "save" money through headcount reduction until after the negotiations, they wouldn't have had the large salary increase that mostly negated the savings from the 10% reduction in headcount.

CHAPTER 8

Eliminating Customers as a Way to Profitability

During the Great Recession, as some have called the 2007 to 2010 period (originally coined by Adam Posen), companies have started to look at the way they do business. They are examining all parts of their products and services in an effort to rationalize their offerings to increase their profit margins. This term "rationalization" is just a fancy term meaning that companies are looking at where they make money and where they lose money across their organization. They are taking apart each function, each job, each service, or each product they offer to clients to determine if it is profitable and if it should be kept in the future, or if it's a loss-maker or a time-distracter to be discarded or sold off. The theory is that they can be a lot more profitable if they concentrate on the things that make money and minimize the things that do not make money.

They are doing what the consultants and economists/educators think is rational. To some extent, this is a good idea. Some good things will come from this. Some companies will be able to charge higher prices for things they practically give away now for free. They will discover new products and services that meet their clients' needs that produce exciting margins the company can live with. Of course, most companies will screw this up. I had one client in the late 1990s that went through the same exercise.

Small Customers Cost a Lot

I was working for a large telecom company in the U.S. that had a weird management philosophy, where for eighteen months all it cared about was increasing revenue, with little concern for profitability. After the initial eighteen-month period, it would start a similar pattern, but it was totally reversed, where all it cared about was profitability, taking the foot off the revenue accelerator. During the profitability cycle, the company frequently did a "customer rationalization." I went through two and a half cycles of this circus before I jumped ship to what I thought would be a better company.

The "customer rationalization" is where a company looks at where its revenue and profits come from (i.e., which group of customers). The company breaks down its base of customers, typically into residential, small and medium businesses (SME), enterprise (really large customers: think Fortune 1000), and wholesale customers (in this case, other telecom companies that bought services to resell to their own clients). They then look at all the functions across the company, like marketing, finance, customer service, and order processing, and do time studies to see how much time of each function the different customer categories take up. Most companies do a similar exercise occasionally to make sure that they are operating efficiently.

This company took it a step too far and wanted to know if it could eliminate the lower-margin customer types and just concentrate on the customers that bring in the greatest margins. On paper and in the consultants' minds, this was a logical step. If the company was concerned about profitability and not revenue, why not eliminate or sell some of the customers to a competitor and receive cash for them? In theory, this should maximize profits.

The problem with this idea in the telecom industry is that the costs of the network tend to be fixed. The more traffic (minutes, Mbps of bandwidth, etc.) you get over this fixed cost, the lower the cost per unit. Simple math can tell you not to do this, but apparently nobody on the management team went beyond fourth grade because they could not do the math.

The management team started looking at customer service and billing and discovered that it cost a lot more to support and produce invoices for a bunch of smaller residential and SME customers than to bill just a few hundred enterprise and wholesale customers. Percentage-wise, based on revenue, it cost almost 10% of the customer's invoice for the average residential and SME customer but only 1.5% for the larger customers.

Then they looked at marketing costs. To market to residential and SME customers, they needed to use mass-market media (TV, radio, print ads, etc). These media sources cost a lot of money to use effectively. You cannot just advertise at 2 a.m., when media costs are practically nothing, and expect to get a lot of customers. Most campaigns cost in the millions to produce and distribute. For enterprise and wholesale customers, marketing costs were almost nonexistent. Except for some glossies, small focus groups, and an occasional meal, there is little marketing done to win enterprise customers. The reason that enterprise customers are not heavily marketed to is because most of the sales are based on RFPs (request for proposal) or one-on-one selling from the sales team (relationship selling). Money would just be wasted if you went out and ran ads during prime-time TV programs to hit your target audience of decision makers.

Management looked at the cost of providing the services for enterprise customers. Since the customers tended to buy in bulk (large bandwidth pipes), the cost per unit was a lot lower. It was just as expensive to maintain a high-bandwidth customer as a low-bandwidth customer calling customer service or working with their network operations to trouble shoot a fault. The only expense that was greater was billing, because the larger customers tended to have larger bills with more services and call records that tended to increase the paper consumption.

In addition to all reductions in the support costs of the different functions, if the company concentrated just on the enterprise and wholesale customers, it could also reduce overall staff levels by up to 50% without affecting service. On the surface, getting rid of residential and SME customers made a lot of sense. If they dug deeper, however, management would quickly realize the savings were illusionary and fleeting. But the company decided to sell off its residential and SME base to another large telecom provider in the U.S.

The minute the company started executing this brilliant strategy, the equation quickly unraveled. It sold its residential and SME customers to a competitor for over $200 million. It sold some other sideline businesses that brought in $10 or $12 million. (These were promising businesses that later grew into some very profitable lines.) It sold off a number of its buildings to the employee pension plan because it wanted cash quicker. The pension plan sold the buildings two years later for almost twice as much as it paid for it. It laid off 25% of its staff and transitioned a further 25% to the businesses it sold off.

The first quarter saw an increase in profit (excluding one-time impacts like selling businesses and buildings and laying off people) by over 50%. Revenue declined 35%. The profit was a factor of lower personnel, less administrative staff, less facilities, less of everything. The second quarter after the transformation, the profit increase was less than the first quarter, and revenue continued its downward descent. This continued for the next eighteen months, before the management was replaced and a new strategy was hatched. The company then flip-flopped and went back to trying to increase revenue at the expense of profits.

What the company failed to see was that a lot of its employees had dual roles––to gain internal efficiencies––where they would support all types of customers. Had the business stopped to look at where its new business came from, it would have found out that a lot of its best salespeople came from roles in which they first started selling in the SME business environment. The company also experienced an increase in cost on a per-unit basis for voice and data services because the company was no longer buying as much bandwidth from suppliers, so the suppliers raised their prices. A lot of the people who were laid off provided some of the key roles that helped support the enterprise customers, but whose roles were also dedicated to the residential and SME customers. Most importantly, the company also eliminated a lot of growing companies that were medium-sized, but would soon be large customers, just because they did not fit the definition of an enterprise customer today.

In hindsight, they screwed up big time. They went from being a top-five carrier in the U.S. to being maybe in the top twenty-five, eight years after the transformation. The final salt in the wound is that the companies that purchased the spun-off businesses are all now in the top ten. I have been tempted to try to follow the future careers of the boneheads who led the change as a rock-solid way of finding out who to short (make money by selling a stock today in anticipation of buying it back cheaper in the future) in the telecom industry. Investment tip: smart money always follows successful management; dumb money, speculators; and short sellers follow the losers.

Lesson to Learn From This Chapter

The lesson from this chapter is that it is generally not a good idea to eliminate a large section of your customer base without a well-thought-out plan on where you want the company to go. Time and time again, businesses today think too short-term. They are so busy trying to appease Wall Street so that they can cash in their options that they forget the truth about businesses. Well-run businesses with consistent growth profiles are always favored over erratic cyclical businesses when it comes to the stock market.

Cyclical businesses tend to have great bursts for short periods of time, but they always disappoint when the cycle turns against them. If CEOs concentrated more on trying to take their businesses in a certain direction, they would make more money over the long run for the company and themselves. More about this in the next chapter.

CHAPTER 9

Short-termitis and the Cost of Poor Management

A problem has been building for a while now in modern business, mostly affecting American, British, and European companies. The problem stems from one of the most basic human traits: greed. Mix that with stupidity and large amounts of cash flowing around the world, and you quickly have a gargantuan problem. The problem is not hunger, resource depletion, or AIDs, but it is equally wasteful and damaging; the problem is Short-termitis. Now, you may ask, "How can Short-termitis be mentioned in the light of such large problems that affect humanity so directly?" The way I see it, more damage is caused to the planet every year from short-term thinking to appease Wall Street than from hunger, resource depletion, and disease. More lives are ruined, more families are split apart, and more economic damage has been done in the name of Short-termitis than by all the hunger, resource depletion, and diseases combined.

I can hear you laughing now. Give me a second to explain why I see it that way. Let's look at AIDS. In the U.S., AIDS and HIV kill over 14,000 people annually, according to the Centers for Disease Control and Prevention. People spend $28 billion per year to treat the disease. AIDS impacts the U.S.

negatively by $14 billion every year through lost work time and other non-medical support costs. While this is serious, I would argue that short-term thinking causes much more damage. Let's compare the annual impact of AIDS with the impact of Robert "Bob" Nardelli when he worked at Home Depot.

Bob was hired in December 2000 to help transform Home Depot to be better positioned to compete against a rapidly growing competitor by the name of Lowe's. Home Depot was starting to hit maturity, and the original management felt it was time to hang up their hats and find a professional manager to run the company and take it in a different direction. At that point, you must applaud the original Home Depot management. They knew their time had come to pass the baton to "professional" management that would take them to the next level. At the time Bob took over (2000), Home Depot had annual revenue of $45.7 billion and pretax profit of $4.2 billion (as reported by the S&P). I am using December 29, 2000, last trading day of 2000, as a before-change date for the price of the shares. They ended the trading day at $39.76. When the board ousted Bob in January 2007, revenues had grown to $77.3 billion, and pretax profit increased to $6.6 billion. January 31, 2007, share price ended at $37.45. By January 30, 2009, the price declined further to $21.07. The market value of the company declined from $105.7 billion to $78.5 billion from the end of 2000 to the end of 2007 (even worse if you look at 2009 numbers). Weighted number of shares, 1.993 billion in February 2007, was a decrease from the 2.352 billion shares in December 2000. Even though the number of shares had decreased roughly 15%, the price still decreased 6% (using 2007 numbers), or a whopping 47% (using 2009 numbers) over a seven- or nine-year period, respectfully. This happened during a time in which the company grew in total revenue, stores, or you-name-it measure. It also coincided with the largest boom in housing and construction that the U.S. has ever seen. So what happened to give a negative return to shareholders over such a long period of time?

Transformation

When Bob took over in 2001, he quickly started to put his imprint on what Home Depot was and his vision on what Home Depot should become. Jumping quickly through steps one and two in the CEO 101 process, Bob initiated a large increase in the dividends paid to shareholders. He also planted the seeds to his two-prong vision: international expansion, and growth through acquisitions in supplying building professionals. In 2001 and 2002, Home Depot purchased Total Home and Del Norte in Mexico to quickly become that country's number one home improvement retailer. Home Depot also purchased Your Other Warehouse to help expand its HD Supply business, a business formed a couple of years prior to supply professional builders and remodelers.

From 2002 to 2004, Home Depot went through the U.S. downturn relatively unscathed. To prop up its stock, it introduced a series of large share buybacks and large dividend payout increases. These measures worked. As the U.S. was emerging from the recession, stock price and sales increased rapidly. Flush with cash from the increased sales, Home Depot went shopping to support Bob's vision on what Home Depot should be. It acquired Home Mart in Mexico, expanded into China, and purchased Creative Touch Interiors (to help expand in the HD Expo design area) and White Cap Construction (to expand into the new field of "do-it-for-me," where you can hire Home Depot to do your project).

Then the Home Depot acquisitions simply exploded. In 2005, Home Depot purchased twenty-one businesses, including Hughes Supply, National Waterworks, Contractor Warehouse, Williams Brothers Lumber, and Chem-Dry. Most of the businesses helped expand HD Supply to become the largest supplier to the professional homebuilder market. It further expanded by opening more HD Expo Design Centers and a couple of retail concept trials, where it entered specialized markets, like flooring. On the international side, it purchased The Home Way chain of home improvement stores in China to further expand into six cities in total.

Starting in 2006, the business cycle turned against Home Depot and Bob Nardelli's expansion plans. The U.S. housing market had just popped the largest bubble that the industry had ever gone through. Signs were showing up around the edges that Home Depot's HD Supply was going to go into revenue and income freefall as a housing cycle hit professional homebuilders and their suppliers extremely hard.

From 2000 to 2006, Home Depot had expanded its workforce from 227,000 to 364,000 employees. In hindsight, the acquisitions and expansion were mostly done at the peak of the housing cycle and, presumably, at peak market prices for the companies purchased.

In January 2007, Home Depot's board decided they had had enough with Bob Nardelli and the direction he was taking the company. They both agreed to part ways (my opinion is that he was fired, but "part ways" sounds so politically correct; yeah, I want to vomit, too). They wished him good luck. "Oh, by the way, what about the money that I was promised?" he wondered. Home Depot's board said, "Oh, about that. If we give you $210 million, will you go away nicely?" Bob had to think it over. "Sure, I can use a nice vacation." So Bob went on his merry way and took a short vacation and then got a job running Chrysler. A few years later, Chrysler went bankrupt. I bet the board at Home Depot was glad to pay the rumored $210 million severance package. It pissed off the shareholders, but I kind of think it was money well spent. Sometimes you just want your problems to go away. Why do you think lawyers cost so much money?

In August 2007, Home Depot sold HD Supply to three private equity companies, with Home Depot maintaining a small portion of the shares (12.5%), while also guaranteeing $1 billion in debt. Home Depot recorded $8.3 billion in proceeds from the sale. They subsequently used these funds and corporate funds/lines of credit to fund $10 billion plus share buyback. After the disposal of HD Supply and retrenchment in store openings, Home Depot's employee ranks shrank to 322,000. Over 40,000 people either left during the selloff of HD Supply or through attrition.

Here are the details of Home Depot since Bob took over, plus two years, since it does still take some time for the new CEO to put his or her stamp on things.

Market value of Home Depot stock, January 29, 2001 *(Annual report shares X Closing price in Yahoo Finance on date or next trade date)*	$105.7 billion
Market value of Home Depot stock, January 28, 2007 *(Annual report shares X Closing price in Yahoo Finance on date or next trade date)*	$78.5 billion
Market value of Home Depot stock, February 1, 2009 *(Annual report shares X Closing price in Yahoo Finance on date or next trade date)*	$35.8 billion
Decline in value of shares from January 2001 to February 2009	-$69.9 billion
Dividends paid from December 2000 to January 2009	+$8.3 billion
Money spent since 2000 purchasing shares (net of sales)	+$24.2 billion
Total debt, December 2000	$1.549 billion
Total debt, February 2007	$11.66 billion
Net increase in debt	-$10.11 billion
Cost of acquisitions	-$8.22 billion
Net proceeds after disposal	+$8.42 billion
Writedown of businesses disposed	-$3.27 billion
Severance package reportedly paid to Mr. Nardelli	-$210 million
Net impact to Home Depot shareholders of poor leadership at Home Depot	-$50.79 billion

I am purposely not showing the profits that Home Depot earned during 2000 to 2007 in the above. Normally, the profits are invested back into the business and do not always accurately reflect the value shareholders gained. These reinvested profits should have resulted in a business that is more valuable over time. Clearly, this did not happen, evidenced by the value that the stock market placed on Home Depot during the period. The loss in market value of the company, even with all the dividends paid and the amount of shares repurchased, showed a decline in what people would purchase the company for based on it being an ongoing concern (i.e., not

deciding to break up the company and sell the parts, or going out of business). Home Depot would have been better off just using the money they
spent on acquisitions, buybacks, and dividends to deposit in a low-interest
bank account (or maybe investing it back in the core business). We will never
know. It is easy for me to second-guess Home Depot's game plan after the
fact. To put this one situation in perspective, I want to compare Home Depot
to HIV/AIDS in the U.S. I know what you are saying: "HIV/AIDS? What type of
sick person would compare a do-it-yourself home repair company that had
a poor result to a deadly disease?" I would.

In the U.S., we currently have approximately 1.2 million people living
with HIV/AIDS, according to a United Nations estimate. Assume each one of
the people living with HIV/AIDS in the U.S. makes the U.S. average GDP per
person of $46,869 (per the IMF), and further assume they miss 25% of their
pay due to time off to treat their ailment ($14.1 billion in lost wages and pro-
ductivity, if you are keeping score at home). If you add in the approximate
$26 billion spent on HIV/AIDS treatments in the U.S., plus the $12.8 billion
the federal government spends on HIV/AIDS programs (non-treatment programs; treatment programs are already in the $26 billion treatment amount),
you get a whopping $52.9 billion spent on supporting people with HIV/AIDS
in the U.S. per year. This is not counting the research that is being conducted
to find a cure. Still, $52.9 billion is a rather large number. The $52.9 billion is
an annual number. The impact to shareholders in Home Depot over eight
years was almost the same as the impact of HIV/AIDS annually.

Comparing the HIV/AIDS annual cost to the U.S. with the damage done
to Home Depot shareholders is to make a point. The point is not that Home
Depot should have fired its CEO and donated money to help HIV/AIDS
patients. The point is that the cost of subpar performance at the executive
level has an extremely large cost. I feel that the average person has gotten so numb to large numbers from hearing them repeatedly on TV that
they needed some way of identifying with them to make them real, hence
the comparison. This is waste on a grand scale. This affects companies, their
employees, the communities where they operate, and anyone with money

invested in the stock market, including mutual funds and 401(k) plans. We cannot eliminate stupidity and greed in the executive suite, but we can look to minimize it. Just think of all the money that could be saved. Remember, this is only one example. I truly believe that there are multiple dozens of examples to be found in the U.S. of similar results of poor management and the waste that it causes in the largest 500 companies alone.

To be fair to Home Depot and Robert Nardelli, I believe that the board shares a lot of the responsibility. They were so concerned about what Wall Street thinks and how they valued the company that they created an environment where Home Depot did a lot of short-term things that had a long-term negative impact. Mr. Nardelli had to have board approval to make the acquisitions, buy back the shares, and take the company in the direction that he presumably wanted the business to go in. In addition, I can actually understand the acquisitions that Home Depot made because one has to remember that the U.S. was caught up in the biggest housing bubble of all time (probably to be repeated by the next largest housing bubble of all time fifteen years from now since history tends to repeat itself). Everybody (well, probably 80% of Americans) thought that house prices would keep on increasing. Naturally, Home Depot saw the increased in demand and went for it. It expanded with new stores and bought out competitors. It purchased companies that it felt were a natural fit or an extension of its current business. Looking back, we can see that it clearly was caught up in the bubble and paid too much.

The point is not to chastise Home Depot or Robert Nardelli. The point is to show that the costs of some short-term actions have long-term impacts. U.S. businesses (and, right now, UK and European businesses) are too focused on appeasing Wall Street and the dumb money that Wall Street throws around that they have forgotten how to run a business for the long-term. I understand if you are turning around a failing company that you need to focus on the current quarter because you might not make it to the next one. For the other 95% of the listed companies, this is simply not the case. If they are so focused on the current quarter, they are doomed to fail in the long run because they are not looking at what is coming down the road. Management and the boards are too concerned about cashing in options today that they lose sight of the larger payday that will happen three to five years from now if they are truly successful and have positioned the company to take advantage of the future business environment.

Short-term Savings Causing Long-term Pain from Outsourcing to China and India

One of the key trends in business today is the transferring of technologies and jobs to China and India. China and India have been growing their economies between 7% to 11% annually for more than a decade. Some of this growth is from domestic sources; as people get wealthier, they tend to spend more money on improving their lives through modern conveniences. The majority of China and India's growth stems from exporting back to the countries that provided the initial technology to them in the first place. It probably would have taken China and India twice as long to develop their high-tech industries if the U.S., and later Europe, did not transfer the information that Chinese and Indian companies needed to build their products and services.

Chinese and Indian businesspeople are extremely smart and focused on the long-term. Their goal is to do what Japan did in the 1970s and 1980s, but only faster. They both have an advantage that Japan has not had since the early 1970s: their labor force is cheap and reasonably well educated. The Chinese and Indians turn out more MBAs and PhDs than all other countries. These newly educated employees are all eager to improve their living conditions. They are willing to do the extra work, knowing they will receive the long-term economic benefit. In addition, the average person in these countries saves more than 20% of his or her annual income.

This widespread transfer of technology and jobs just to save a few dollars today is going to come back to bite a lot of U.S., UK, and European businesses in the ass. They are providing their future competitors with information on how to beat them at their own game. I predict (not much of a prediction) that China will surpass the U.S. in GDP sometime in the next fifteen to twenty years. I applaud the Chinese and Indians for their effort. They should be rewarded for all the work they are doing to get to the next level. History has shown time and time again that superpowers get complacent. They do not want to put forth the extra effort that is needed to advance society. They eventually are overtaken by a rival who is willing to go the extra mile. Americans and Europeans need to get off their butts if they want to keep up with China and India. If they don't, they will fall way behind and suffer a slow erosion of their way of life and their standard of living.

I predict (I do not need much of a crystal ball to see this one happening) that unless U.S. and European companies start making dramatic changes to how they think about the future, things will go into a continuous long-term decline. I know that this prediction was also made in the 1980s when Japan was charging ahead, but this time it is different. In the 1980s, and for the most part, the 1960s to the 1980s, Japanese business was at its pinnacle. The companies and the country were growing so strongly that most American companies and people felt that it was only a matter of time before the Japanese bought out all American companies. The growth in Japanese companies also masked a structural weakness that they had. Japan was an expensive place to live and conduct business. The costs of living in Japan were so great that many families chose to have only one child or none at all. This led to a slowing of demographic growth and a rapid graying of the population. As an expensive society grows older and older, there are fewer and fewer young people propping up the retired folks. A smaller amount of youth also slows innovation and change, because youth is aggressive and is not bothered by history.

Unlike Japan, China and India have large low-paid populations that are young and want to work and change the world. The sheer size of this eager young group of people will lead to large changes in their and our societies. Youth will change the world. China alone has over 300 million people who are below the age of fourteen. India has more than 350 million in the same age group. This represents over 10% of the world's total population––and in just those two countries––below the age of fourteen. If you couple this with the lower incomes that are earned in China and India versus the Western world, you have a great motivational factor that will lead to dramatic change. These young people will all want to do things differently than their parents. They will strive for better lives. They will want more modern conveniences. They will buy their first cars, live in their own houses, watch their own TVs, and eat their own foods. This will be an upsetting trend, where eventually growth will be led out of the East even though the West is currently richer.

This will be the largest transfer of wealth in the history of man. The West will probably experience a stagnation at best, or an outright decline in living standards in some countries. The East will see a rapid ascent to the middle class. Eventually, China and India will do what Japan and Taiwan did previously; they will transform their industries from low-quality cheap producers to become true world-class companies leading their fields. The Western world should not be scared of this change. They should embrace it and look for ways to capitalize on this trend.

Lesson to Learn From This Chapter

Remember, Home Depot is only one company. There are literally dozens like it making short-term decisions that hamper their long-term prospects. This is quite likely a multi-hundred-billion-dollar-a-year problem that society bears. Businesspeople and average Joes all complain about the size of governmental waste, but few complain about some of the boneheads running businesses today throughout the world and their bad cases of Short-termitis.

Short-termitis is, in my opinion, the worst thing happening to businesses today. If companies thought long term, China and India would have taken a lot longer to develop to be two of the leaders in business today. This will have extreme repercussions for the U.S. and Europe in future generations. The Chinese and Indians are extremely smart and patient and have a long-term focus. China will eventually become the largest economy on the planet, and the U.S. will be relegated to a role similar to that of Russia, a has-been superpower talking about its glory days.

CHAPTER 10

Paying Your CEOs as if They Are in the Top Three in the Industry Even Though They Suck (Stock Options for the Masses)

CEO pay escalation has become a hot topic as of late. Some of it is simply pure jealousy and resentment. I know I get pissed when I see some guy (or gal) make $100 million for one year's worth of work. I mostly get pissed at myself for picking the wrong industry and, most of all, not taking the ass-kissing lessons so many years back. But in all seriousness, people do get jealous when they see someone they do not have high regard for make serious big bucks even though they do not own the company. There is also a more valid reason to be upset about current CEO pay. It seems that their pay is going up while the rest of the workers' pay is stagnant at best. Before you label me some kind of bleeding heart liberal (why is their heart always bleeding? I am not sure, but it always is for some reason), I do believe that some of the CEOs who get some of these oversized compensation packages truly earn the money. Now, I know what you are thinking, "He is waffling and can't find a position." Hear me out. I have reasons why they should not be paid that much and also reasons why a **select** few should be paid the large amount, if not more.

CEO pay has been increasing for the last couple of decades at the highest rates on record, in relation to pay for the average employee. In 1980, the average CEO of an S&P 500 company was paid forty-two times what the average American worker earned. In 1990, the average CEO pay increased to one hundred seven times that of the average American worker. In 2000, it peaked at an astonishing five hundred twenty-five times the average American worker's earnings. This number has since dropped to a still eye-popping three hundred forty-four times in 2007.

The numbers do not tell the whole story. Remember, the stats show the average pay of CEOs from the top five hundred companies in the U.S. While the numbers seemed skewed, there are multiple reasons for these dramatic differences. One of the reasons for this change is that starting in 1980 a lot of our higher-earning manufacturing jobs started being replaced with lower-paying service-oriented jobs as manufacturing was deemphasized. Since 1980, a fair portion of those manufacturing jobs was exported to lower-cost manufacturing areas as global trade opened up. While this sucked for a lot of workers in the Midwest, a heavy manufacturing area, it was a boon for a lot of city workers in the coastal areas. It allowed Americans to buy a lot of things more cheaply, and it expanded our standard of living more than before global trade was opened up. The bad news is that it allowed Americans to buy a lot of cheap plastic crap that accumulated in our basements and garages until they could dispose of it. It also allowed Americans to gorge themselves and buy a lot of stuff on credit that they are still paying for today even if the item is long gone.

In addition to the global trade argument, there is the fact that a lot of our S&P 500 companies are now financial, pharmaceutical, or tech companies. In 1980, a lot of these companies simply did not exist. Think of companies like Microsoft (a small business at the time) and Google. The finance companies that did exist were more regulated, and the flow of capital was a lot less, hence the lower revenue and profits. Finance, pharmaceutical, and tech companies do not have the structural costs (factories, inventories, etc.) of the old manufacturing companies. These companies have highly paid workers, but it takes a lot less of them to produce $1 in revenue than it does for a manufacturer. Because these companies are more efficient and profitable, they can afford to pay their executive teams more. As these three industries grew, their share of the S&P 500 became larger and larger, thus skewing the numbers.

Another reason for these high numbers is Walmart. Back in 1980, Walmart only had roughly $1.2 billion in annual sales and only had 21,000 employees. In 1980, GM was the world's largest company with $66 billion in revenue and had its peak number of U.S. employees at over 618,000. Today, Walmart is the world's largest company, with annual sales of $401 billion dollars. It is also now the U.S's largest employer with over 1.4 million employees, while GM only has 80,000 employees in the U.S. as of July 2009. As part of its bankruptcy in 2009, it is looking to reduce the number of employees even further to 55,000 to 60,000 workers. GM's revenue in 2008 was $149 billion. A GM worker makes multiple times more than what a Walmart worker makes. That is one of the reasons Walmart can keep its prices so low. When you add 1.398 million workers over thirty years, earning about 25% of what an average auto company worker earns, thus you start to skew the average income level of the country especially since they are the largest employer in the country. We replaced high paying manufacturing jobs with lower paying retail jobs. This factor helps explain some of the increase in the average income of an S&P 500 CEO versus the average employee (when taken as a multiple of the average employee salary).

Finally, the average CEO pay for an S&P 500 company has increased nominally since 1980. From 1980 to 2006 (latest numbers I have), average CEO compensation for an S&P 500 company has increased six-fold to $15.06 million dollars. During the same period, the median U.S. household income only increased to $48,201 from $17,710, or 2.7 times the level of 1980, versus six times for CEO compensation. If the pay of the average employee is adjusted for inflation, it has stayed static for the time period, while the average S&P 500 CEO's pay increased by a factor of ten. Some researchers try to show the link between the salary increasing to compensate for the size of company by market share that the CEO now runs. I think some of the numbers are skewed because the S&P 500 list has been repeatedly changed as companies grow, shrink, get purchased, merge, or go bankrupt. That means you always have the top 500 CEOs even though almost all of the CEOs of 1980 are long gone. This is the equivalent of having to pay for the top five hundred players in baseball and comparing it to the entire universe of people playing baseball for a living (major and minor leagues). Making an educated guess, I'd guess you would have similar stats on pay increase if you did the top five hundred baseball comparison. I also wonder if they had a similar issue from 1950 to 1980, during a time when supposedly average employee income made nominal progress against inflation because of America's growth during that period.

In addition, the statistics are skewed to be heavily based on stock options, which can typically make up around 60% of CEO pay packages. The statistics are skewed because of the nature of stock options. Typically, a CEO will try to cash in stock options that either have the most value or that are due to soon expire. If a company has a great year because the industry is experiencing an up cycle, a lot of stock options will be cashed. Conversely, if the industry that the CEO is in is having a down cycle, the CEO will only cash in options that are about to expire or if he or she has some obligation to meet. Look at 2005 and 2006, and look at the amount of options cashed in by the homebuilders and mortgage/banking companies' CEOs. It was the peak of the cycle for their industry, and they took advantage of the high stock prices to make some money. Then, in 2007 and 2008, the oil and energy companies' CEOs cashed in big time. This simply means that the options will always skew the results since different industries are in different parts of their cycles, and the CEOs are taking advantage of it. Spread that over only five hundred people, and there is a great chance of skewing the numbers. For example, look at 2000 to 2005. CEO pay peaked in 2000 because of the bull market and dropped through 2003 with the bear market as fewer CEOs cashed in lower numbers of options.

In my opinion, the average stats are skewed also because of the nature of what is being reported. Historically, the top 10% of the people in **anything**, business, sports, finance, etc., make 90% of the money. In business, the top 10% are really the S&P 500 companies when it comes to size. By definition, the S&P 500 is the top five hundred companies in the U.S., ranked by revenue. When you are the biggest, you tend to attract the best and pay for it. Look at the New York Yankees. They are the largest baseball team when it comes to revenue. They also pay the highest so that they can attract the top talent. When that top talent gets too old, they trade them away to find the newest top players, and they pay the new current top dollar for them. If you compare that to the Milwaukee Brewers, a team that has a smaller fan base, they have to grow their talent through their farm system and scouting to find some diamonds in the rough. Unfortunately, as soon as they find some of the best players, they usually lose them when their contracts are up to ball clubs with bigger budgets that can afford to pay the higher salaries.

Top 3 in the Industry

Enough about the average CEO pay package for S&P 500 executives—let's talk smack about the average CEOs in the U.S. who get paid well for subpar service. There seems to be a belief across American business that you can make an average CEO better by paying him or her as if he or she is one of the top three CEOs in the industry. To me, this is sort of like the issue where Wall Street makes a bunch of crappy subprime mortgage loans to people who can't afford to pay for them and then divides up the risk between super crappy and just plain crappy and calls the plain crappy loans strong and rates them AAA. Where I come from, crap is crap; there are no different grades. Similar to CEOs, no matter what you pay people, if they are crappy at their jobs, they will always be crappy. The only thing that changes is that you now have someone who is crappy **and** overpaid. Great, how is that going to help anyone? It doesn't. But then, why does this happen?

It happens because boards of directors are made up of human beings. Like all human beings, some have strong traits and some have weaknesses. Outside of the S&P 500, or in the minor leagues (to keep with an earlier metaphor), boards are not always made up with the best people for the job. A lot of the boards on smaller companies are packed with relatives, friends of key shareholders, prominent former politicians, business school professors, and anybody with money or on the periphery of the business world that can fog a mirror. These people all have great intentions. For the most part, they want to find the best people for the job. Not knowing the correct people or having a big enough name to attract the best in the industry, they turn to a headhunting consultant, and this is where it all starts.

Headhunting consultants have their work cut out for them. They have to balance the requests to get a competent person in a small company while maximizing the prospective CEO's salary. Why are the headhunters so worried about getting the highest salary for a new CEO? Money! The headhunter gets a percentage of the first-year salaries (and packages, sometimes) for everyone they place. These percentages range from 10% to as high as 25%. This is **big** money. Imagine placing a person who earns $1 million a year at, say, only a 10% fee. The headhunter gets a cool $100K for his or her work. Sounds like a lot to me, but like all profit-motivated people, they want to earn more. So how do you do that? You convince the naïve board that if they want to have a company that is in the top three in the industry, they need to pay their top "talent" so that their package falls in the top three. To do this, the headhunter does an industry CEO pay survey and finds that the top three in the industry all earn above $15 million per year. So instead of making $100K, he or she can earn $1.5 million for doing a little more work.

Like in most major league sports, these headhunters act like agents for their talent. They constantly try to place their best performers with different companies every few years so that they can make more money. This leads to CEO pay inflation. If the CEO was successful or got lucky and had a great year, he or she will approach the board about making sure that he or she stays in the top three. More than likely, the top three paid CEOs in the industry will have changed as more and more CEOs are replaced. The pay bar continues to rise unless the industry has a downturn, or boards or shareholders balk at the pay packages their CEOs make. Usually it is the former rather than the latter that stops the increase until the next upturn in the industry.

Now that I have written about people who really probably do not truly deserve their pay packages, let's give some examples of people who truly deserve the large packages they get.

CEOs Who Deserve Their Pay Packages

Without trying to sound like I have a man crush or something, I will go over four individuals that I really respect for their investment prowess. All four are CEOs or legendary investors. They are not really known for their styles of managing people but for their money and business management skills. The four individuals are Wilbur Ross, Jack Welch, Jeff Immelt, and Jim Rogers. Two are very successful managers and two are successful money managers. All four are self-made individuals. They all have a couple of common traits. First and foremost, they are contrarians. They look for inefficiencies in stocks or businesses due to market or cycle forces, and purchase them in anticipation of future value (the definition of buying low and selling high). They look for ways to identify future opportunities, like a fortune-teller looks into a crystal ball. They all have the tenacity to stick with their plans even when they are perceived as wrong about an investment or a business, a fact that in most cases makes them want to invest or expand even more.

Now it may seem like I am kissing a little butt in the next sections, but I want to clarify something. I do not always agree with their moves, but I really look up to them as heroes. They are the embodiment of what most Americans think of as a heroic American. They are seen as tough men with a wide streak of individualism. They are wildly successful even though most people thought they were wrong or strange when they started out. They have been counted out multiple times in the past, but they always seem to find a way to come back stronger than ever. The only things they are missing are the Stetsons and a horse named "Trigger" (at least to the investment geek crowd).

Wilbur Ross

Wilbur Ross came from an upper middle-class background. His father was a lawyer and his mother a teacher. He attended Yale for undergrad and Harvard for his MBA. Even though he is Ivy League-educated, I will not hold that against him. While at Yale, he edited a literary magazine. I think it is there that he first learned to be an independent thinker.

Wilbur went to Wall Street in the mid-1970s to make his fortune. He first got started with Rothschild Investments, LLC. He worked his way through Rothschild to become a leading expert in bankruptcies. In the late 1980s through the early 1990s, he spent time cleaning up failed companies that the junk bond mess left behind after Drexel Burnham failed. I assume it was then that he learned an extremely valuable lesson: sometimes there is more money to be made cleaning up something after the fast money has left. He learned that you can swoop in and pick up quality assets for pennies on the dollar when everybody wants to wash their hands of a fallen company or a downtrodden industry.

In 1997, he was promoted within Rothschild to run a private equity fund, where he specialized in buying companies out of bankruptcies. After three years running the fund, he felt that he wanted to go out on his own and not be constrained by working for a larger company. He founded WL Ross & Co, LLC, in 2000 with $450 million in investor money.

After 9/11, Wilbur used his valuable bankruptcy experience and applied it to the steel industry. Throughout the 1980s, 1990s, and the early 2000s, the steel industry was in a long secular decline. As more and more manufacturing capacity was closed down in the U.S. and shipped overseas, there was less and less need for steel in the U.S. That, coupled with a formerly large unionized work force that had generous benefits packages with more retir-ees than workers, left the steel industry in a detrimental state. Excluding U.S. Steel and Nucor, there really were not any properly functioning companies that were not being kept alive by either government support or bank loans tied to assets (at junk bond yields routinely in the high teens).

When the 2001 to 2002 recession hit, it took the last remaining hopes that the industry could survive without widespread bankruptcies. Wilbur saw his opportunity and formed International Steel Group (ISG). Starting in April 2002, ISG acquired Bethlehem, LTV, Weirton, Acme, Georgetown, and part of U.S. Steel. Many of the companies that were purchased were acquired in bankruptcy, thus eliminating a lot of the debt, pension, and union benefit liabilities, and lowering the structural operating cost. ISG became the larg-est steel company in the U.S. ISG was later bought out by Mittal Steel; the combined company is the largest integrated steel company throughout the world. From the reports that I have read, WL Ross & Co still owns its shares in Mittal and is one of the top shareholders in Mittal Steel. Wilbur's initial $325 million investment in 2001 grew to $4.5 billion dollars when it was bought out by Mittal Steel.

In late 2004, WL Ross & Co created International Coal Group (ICG; man, does his firm like the name "international," as you will see it is in almost every company he owns) to purchase three coal companies out of bankruptcy. Wilbur's efforts to purchase additional coal companies seems to have been delayed by the run up in coal prices starting in 2005 that coincided with the commodities bull market. I am sure that once the market dives or some firms get into trouble, ICG will be there to purchase them.

In 2005, WL Ross & Co turned its attentions to the automotive Indus-try just as that industry started showing signs of weakness. It created International Automotive Components (IAC) to acquire automotive parts manufacturers around the world. It initially purchased all of Collins & Aikman's European operations and the interior plastics division of Lear. Wilbur's company also bought out 77% of Safety Component International. I suspect, with the automotive industry (2009) going through major bouts of bankruptcies, that we will see IAC acquiring additional part manufacturers, if not divisions of some of the auto manufacturers.

Then, in 2007, during the bursting of the housing bubble and the subsequent mortgage meltdown and credit crisis, WL Ross & Co started buying mortgage-servicing companies specializing in subprime mortgages. Wilbur purchased American Home Investment Corp's mortgage servicing platform and mortgage servicing rights after the company filed for bankruptcy. He also purchased Option One from H&R Block for $1.1 billion in 2008. Later on, the company purchased a large mortgage portfolio from Citigroup when that lender got into trouble and had to be bailed out by funds from the U.S. government. These, plus a couple of additional timely purchases while the world was panicking and running away from subprime mortgages, allowed WL Ross & Co to become the largest third-party loan servicer in the U.S. Before the mortgage fiasco is over, I would not be surprised if WL Ross & Co offers to help bail out the U.S. Government and take over the subprime lending of troubled agency lenders like Fannie Mae or Freddie Mac.

In 2008 and 2009, WL Ross & Co started investing in municipal bond insurers and banks (one of the first private equity firms to do so). With a lot of banks being taken over by the FDIC, I fully expect to see more reports of takeovers by WL Ross & Co. In my opinion, the last three years' worth of acquisitions look like he is trying to create a major financial institution that spans mortgages, banking, and insurance. If he can do it with a minimum amount of debt, which––unlike the rest of the private equity companies–– he is famous for, he will come out of the mess many more times wealthier. He is now in his early seventies. I would not be surprised if, by the time he turns eighty, he is vying to be atop the Forbes 400 list.

Jack Welch (and later Jeff Immelt)

Where to start with this duo? Let's start at the beginning. Jack Welch started with General Electric (GE) in 1960 as a junior engineer. Jack worked his way up the company ladder during the 1960s and '70s. By 1972, Jack had obtained a vice president position within GE. In 1977, he was promoted to senior vice president. Jack took over as CEO and chairman of the conglomerate in 1981, the youngest in the company's history. At the time, in the early 1980s, there was a general trend where conglomerates were being broken apart due to the lower value Wall Street placed on conglomerates versus singularly focused companies.

When Jack took over as CEO in 1981, GE was only making about $27 billion a year in revenue. When Jack left GE in 2001, GE was making almost $140 billion a year in revenue. The market cap had increased twenty-nine times (from approximately $14 billion to over $410 billion). The growth in revenue and market cap do not tell the entire story, they just recount statistics like some old baseball cards. You cannot get the feel for what Jack Welch accomplished without digging deeper into how he did it and how he changed American business along the way.

In 1981, GE was a hodgepodge of companies loosely assembled around industries with an electrical and manufacturing motif. GE was a lumbering giant. It had over 400,000 employees in the early '80s. It made hundreds of different products, mostly of mediocre quality. It lacked focus and a plan for where it was going. Most people thought that its future was not bright. Upon taking the reins, Jack changed the company radically. He created a policy that for every business that GE was in, GE had to be number one or two in that industry. Divisions that did not meet this requirement were disposed of or were expanded through acquisitions to become number one or two. By 1985, GE had shed so many divisions and laid off so many people that the number of employees had shrunk by over 25% to only 299,000.

Jack did not just stop with making cuts. He expanded into new areas that he felt had long-term potential. In 1986, he purchased NBC (one the largest TV networks in the U.S.) to expand into the media industry. He later purchased Universal to create a media powerhouse. In addition to expanding into media, he also spent heavily on finance and healthcare, two industries poised for serious long-term growth given the needs of the baby boomer generation. He felt that baby boomers needed access to finance to support their upwardly mobile desires to purchase homes, cars, and stuff on credit. GE became a leader in credit cards, insurance, and home mortgages. GE Capital, the finance division, became the largest part of the entire GE operation. He also recognized the need to be part of the healthcare industry. Major advances in healthcare, due to regularly advancing computers and technology in the 1980s, held the promise to grow to be a large division of GE. Already being a technology leader in advanced electronics for aircraft, weapons, and appliances, it was a logical extension for GE to expand into healthcare technology. As more and more people were living longer, they created a natural need for more and more advances in healthcare. Combining the demographic need with advanced electronics prowess, GE was able to profitably expand into this industry.

A lot of the success GE had was in hiring and developing the best people. GE Capital was led by the brilliant Gary Wendt. A lot of people contend that Gary was mostly responsible for GE Capital's meteoric rise in revenues and profits. I would agree that Gary did the lion share of the work at GE Capital, but it was Jack's persistence in getting, developing, and maintaining the best people for each role that lead to hiring and promoting Gary. He gave Gary the tools and support to be successful.

If the story were just one division's success, then I would be writing just about Gary Wendt. It was the fact that GE has hired and developed so many top managers across so many different industries that it could not just be a fluke. Jack was so focused on developing talent that he deployed a lot of different techniques. It was rumored that he would routinely fire the bottom 10% of managers annually. He was one of the first to deploy Six Sigma (covered in an earlier chapter). Two of his top three managers have gone on to lead GE or other major S&P 500 companies (Jeff Immelt, who I discuss in the next section; and James McNerney, CEO of 3M corporation, just to name a few).

Jack also learned how to manage Wall Street. Jack knew that money managers had to show consistent results over the long run or they would lose their jobs. To be successful on Wall Street, managers would look for companies that had predictable streams of revenues and profits that both continually showed an upward path. To encourage Wall Street to favorably view GE's stock, he had to deliver consistent and long-term growth so that the money managers would want to purchase the shares of GE. To do this, he turned to two different mechanisms. He would always have a deal pending where he could sell a division or company at a profit if he needed a one-time boost to make a quarterly number. He would also have GE Capital manage its receivables and short-term investments so that, in a pinch, it could get him over a hurdle if there appeared to be a chance that GE would miss a quarterly number.

Some people felt that he would manufacture earnings so that he would always make his number and thus, presumably, increase the value of GE shares. The way I look at this concern about GE's performance was that, at the time, this was perfectly legal. He did not just use one-time gains occasionally; he perfected it. He just took what Wall Street wanted, and he consistently delivered; thus his share price consistently increased. After Jack left, the SEC changed the rules so that companies could not manipulate their earnings as easily as they did in the past. Some argue that if Jack were running a company today, he could not have the same success. I would argue that like any great coach or visionary, he had the ability to see the big picture and to manage his team to obtain the desired end result using any means necessary given the current rules. He viewed the rules as guidelines and looked for ways that others had not thought of to take advantage of his current situation. In an ever-changing business environment, these traits are still highly desirable.

Some people would also argue that Jack Welch was extremely lucky, catching a super cycle in the stock market. It is true that the period from 1982 to 2000 was one of the greatest, if not **the** greatest, bull-run of all time in the stock market. Would Jack have been as successful today as he was when he took over 1982? It is certainly debatable. My counter to this is that he did have the luck of getting in at the beginning of a long upward trend, but so did thousands of other CEOs. Each and every one of the CEOs brought in around the same time that Jack took over GE had the same set of market circumstances that he had, yet very few had the vision to control the destiny as well as Jack did. Sure, he had the advantage of a super cycle, the ability to control GE's earnings, and the resources of the mighty GE itself, but it was the vision that put everything together. Look at all the top companies that had similar market conditions. Look at GM, look at Sears, look at AT&T. All of them have faltered to some degree. They all lacked vision and willpower to make the necessary changes that time dictates. If GE had done what GM did, they, too, would have gone bankrupt. They chose a longer-term path that was hard to conquer at first, but it became easier as they became a better company. GE could have stayed in appliances, electrical motors, and other bits and pieces, but we would probably be talking about a company that would barely be in the S&P 500 or that would have been bought out decades ago. Instead, Jack rose to the occasion and, as they say, the rest is history. In my opinion, a great leader or investor will rise to the top in spite of the current market conditions, while everybody else just bitches and moans. This is truly what separates the great from the rest of us.

Jeff Immelt

In some ways, Jeff had a harder job than when Jack Welch took over GE. He was the next CEO on watch after the enormously successful rein of Jack Welch. He had the world watching him, just looking for the time when he made a mistake. In addition to the intense scrutiny that Jeff had, he also had to contend with something Jack never did––new SEC rules that forbade the manipulation of earnings.

Jack Welch innovated a lot of the ways that were now shunned by the SEC. Jack utilized the financial arm to do many last-minute deals where he would buy and sell businesses on the final days of different quarters to help make the quarterly numbers expected by Wall Street. The predictability of GE's earnings made it a top choice for mutual funds. They all clamored to own GE's rapidly appreciating shares. This long-term consistent growth led the share price to be arguably overvalued. This overvaluing of the shares prior to Jeff taking over made it almost a certainty that GE would decline in value when management changed.

So far during Jeff's tenure, GE revenues grew from $140 billion to their current $182 billion. While revenue growth was not as spectacular as it was under Jack Welch's rein as CEO, it still has been impressive in its own right. When you are dealing with a large company like GE, the law of large numbers catches up with you. It is easier to double your revenue when you are making $1 billion per year than when you are making $100 billion per year. To put this in perspective, the approximately $42 billion in revenue growth under Jeff is like adding a company ranked fifty-third on the S&P 500 list. There are only fifty-two companies in America that have more revenue than $42 billion per year.

Most recently, Jeff has had to contend with the Great Recession that impacted the profitability of GE Capital due to the write-downs for losses on loans. He has also had to do something that Jack never had to do––he has had to shrink GE's balance sheet. GE, under Jeff, got into a little bit of an issue where it expanded its balance sheet too fast due to growth in GE Capital. To cover this faster-than-cash-flow expansion, it had to take on some additional debt. Like most financial companies, it made the classic mistake of borrowing short and lending long. It had to turn to the U.S. government to get some help in selling commercial paper so that it did not get squeezed during the credit crunch. This bailout led the major ratings companies to lower GE's debt ranking level from the vaulted AAA that it had held since 1958. GE has taken some measures to increase capital and has been working to pare down its short-term debt levels.

Growing $42 billion in annual revenue within nine years, and dealing with a major recession, a drying up of a major liquidity source (commercial paper), and a rating downgrade has set Jeff Immelt apart from most managers. Very few CEOs would have been able to grow this much revenue in a short period of time or deal with such a major issue where tens of billions of dollars of debt had to be rolled over within months during a liquidity crisis. To be able to still succeed, given the issues GE has had to contend with, especially while being under a microscope after taking the reins from a business legend, sets Jeff apart from all others.

Jim Rogers

Jim Rogers is, by far, my favorite manager of money. He is everything I aspire to be in the business world. He is an individualist, a contrarian, a sooth-sayer of macroeconomic trends, stubborn and tenacious when he thinks he is correct, and a thrill seeker to boot. He has a long history spanning to the 1970s in spotting and calling long-term directions in multiple different mar-kets from stocks, bonds, currencies, foreign markets, and commodities. He does not restrict himself to only one type of investment vehicle. He pursues whatever investment vehicle he feels will reward him the most in the future.

In 1970, he cofounded the world-famous Quantum fund with George Soros. The Quantum fund was one of the original hedge funds that was set up to take advantage of "special situations." The fund was so successful that it grew a reportedly 4200% over the ten years that Jim was involved with it. The fund became the base for both George Soros's and Jim Roger's large fortunes. After ten years with the fund, Jim decided he had enough and retired at the early age of thirty-eight.

In 1990, he decided he wanted to see more of the world firsthand and at a local level, so he purchased a motorcycle and drove it around the world. He spent two years driving over 65,000 miles by himself through six conti-nents, stopping in dozens of countries along the way. Unlike most tourists, who just want to see the sights and take a few pictures, Jim did the trip with a decidedly business bent. He visited dozens of stock exchanges and met with local listed companies to look for possible investments. He also talked to a lot of local businessmen just to get a better feel for the local business environments. He did this just so he could find investments that Wall Street and other money managers would not find until many years later. He was also brave enough to travel through multiple war zones and to put money to work in many countries that the typical American could not locate on the map. He also liked to invest in postwar economies because he noticed that they tended to have some of the fastest growth, and he could make a kill-ing after the literal killing had stopped. He wrote a book called *Investment Biker*, detailing the trials and tribulations of this epic journey throughout the world. If you ever want an exciting business book to read, this is the one.

A few years later, in 1996, he met his future wife, Paige Parker, during a speaking engagement. During their first date, he asked her if she wanted to take a trip with him around the world. Man, what a way to impress a woman, asking her to go around the world with you. Either you are going to score major brownie points or you are going to be shot down and looked at as some kind of nut job. Luckily for him, Paige was intrigued and agreed to go on the trip. Instead of choosing to do the latest trip on the back of a bike or on a bike of her own, they decided to do it in a Mercedes Benz. My guess is that she thought, "Why be uncomfortable for over 100,000 miles on a bike when I can ride in style?" At least I hope so, since they chose a girly car. They went with an SLK 320, the cute little sports car typically marketed to women. To make matters even worse, they chose a nice bright yellow color. To make it more manly, Jim had the drive train changed to four-wheel drive with a diesel engine. So, now instead of having a cute little chick car, they had a made-over yellow butch lesbian Mercedes Benz 4X4 that doubled as a hardtop convertible. Everywhere they went, they stood out in the crowd.

They started their drive in Iceland in December 1998 and finished in New York in January 2002. During this world-record-setting journey, they managed to cover over 100,000 miles and 116 countries, not to mention dozens of stock exchanges. To top that all off, they arranged their wedding while travelling. This in itself is no small task. If you have ever tried to help your wife to arrange a wedding, it is always a major undertaking. At least your future wife has the advantage of being at home with a phone and the Internet plus local shops to try stuff on or taste items on the menu. Paige had to arrange their wedding while traveling in a car across Europe. Imagine the fights they must have had on that part of the trip! The wife and I argue about what highway we should take while traveling on vacation. I can't imagine my wife and I taking a trip of 100,000 miles **and** me telling her she needs to plan the wedding while we are driving. I do not think we would have gotten married. It shows just how far a woman will go for a chance to marry a man with a convertible Mercedes. I am surprised Mercedes has not tried to use that in an ad! After getting married, they proceeded to "honeymoon" in over a hundred and ten other countries over the next three years.

To recount the trip with Paige through even more countries than his first around-the-world trip, Jim wrote the book *Adventure Capitalist*. *Adventure Capitalist* is every bit as entertaining as his first book. Unlike most Americans, Jim is exceptionally well-traveled and spots trends, business and political, well in advance of almost all investors. The international insight you can gain from reading these two books are invaluable to any investor or citizen of the world.

Jim went on to later call two additional macroeconomic trends, commodities and the growth in China, in his next two books, *Hot Commodities* and *A Bull in China*. In *Hot Commodities*, Jim detailed the coming super cycle in commodities about two years prior to its start. He was so convinced of this upcoming super cycle that he started Rogers International Commodities Index. The index is designed to track multiple different commodities, from energy and metals to agriculture. Since its inception in 1998, it has returned over 470% up to June 2008 (dropping to almost 200% at the end of July 2009).

Jim is also so convinced, like I am, of Asia's (specifically China's) long-term growth trend that he sold his townhouse in Manhattan so that he could move his family to Singapore so that he and his family can be closer to the countries that will lead the next century. He is forecasting, like others, that China will overtake the U.S. to become the superpower of the twenty-first century. History shows that there typically is a changeover in top ranking once a century. In the nineteenth century, England was the predominant country economically, and in the twentieth century, that changed to the present leading country, the U.S. The twenty-first century looks like it belongs to China. He is so convinced that China will be the leader of the twenty-first century that he is making sure that his children learn to speak Mandarin as well as English.

His conviction to follow, at such extremes, and profit from what he feels are likely macroeconomic trends really shows how much he stands out from the crowd. Normally, guys like Jim take their initial success and go and find a nice quiet hobby and a place to kick up their feet and sit back and relax in retirement. Jim's desire to take traveling and investing to such large extremes shows how committed he is to his fields of study. This over-the-top approach to investing gets way above-average results. He has consistently been right about large macroeconomic trends since the 1970s; few have records that even come close. The ones who do are legendary, like Warren Buffett and Bill Gross. I feel that Jim Rogers sits squarely with this bunch.

Lesson to Learn From This Chapter

The lesson from this chapter is that paying a high price does not mean you always get high performance. Most people take shortcuts to performance that usually wind up biting them in the ass. Like the old saying goes, "You cannot have one baby in a month by impregnating nine women." What that means to me is that you cannot rush performance; it is something that is built over time. Paying somebody a higher salary or bonus does not necessarily change the performance that a person accomplishes. If it did, then that person's work ethic would be in question and should not be counted on for long-term results. A person might work harder or more hours, but that does not necessarily mean that the end result, when it comes to management of people or money, would improve. Paying someone $1 million per year should elicit the same performance as paying someone $5 million if he or she is truly a star and is already in charge.

I did not include Warren Buffett in my list for two reasons. The first is that so much has already been written about Warren that I did not feel that I had much more to add on the subject. And secondly, a lot of what I had to say about Wilbur Ross and Jim Rogers was very similar to how I would have praised Warren. To repeat myself would wind up boring my readers.

CHAPTER 11

Wasting Millions on Consultants When the People One Management Layer Down Really Know How to Fix the Problem for Free

This chapter is near and dear to my heart. I have operated as a consultant in the telecom industry for the last seven years in Canada, Europe, the Caribbean, and the South Pacific. Coming into a new assignment, there is always an air of trying to learn how a company operates and who the key players are. One thing I hope that sets me apart from most consultants is my specialty, pricing, for which few people have a fully qualified set of skills. It is hard to copy what does not exist within the companies that I currently work with. That does not mean I don't get advice from the people already working for the company. And here lies the issue. Some consultants have a habit of taking shortcuts and just rehashing information that staff a few management layers down in the company that they are consulting for already know, and they claim it to be their own.

I once worked as a manager for a large U.S. Internet service provider (ISP) in the mid- to late '90s. During this period, the Internet was being reborn and redefined almost monthly. As with new industries, there are few experts, and those who are considered experts are really people who just happened to be in the right place at the right time and got a *few* months' exposure to something new. People were continuously leaving the ISP that I worked for and getting hired to work with large consulting companies like Anderson Consulting, Bain, IBM, and Booz Allen Hamilton. They were easily doubling and sometime tripling their salaries because there were so few "experts" and so many companies trying to hire them. I was too stupid to take up such opportunities even though some were offered. I stayed with the company, waiting until 1999 to transfer overseas to work throughout the Caribbean. Before leaving to sip rum drinks under palm trees (truth is that I still worked too many hours while there and barely got a tan), I got to work with the consultants that my ISP brought in, thus giving me great insight on the quality of these so-called experts.

In 1998, the ISP I worked for merged with another ISP to form the second-largest ISP in the U.S. As part of the merger came the inevitable swarm of the highest paid per-hour-earning opportunists that the world has ever seen. They had armies of consultants from four of the five top consulting companies in North America. Hundreds of consultants took up residence in every available seat and conference room in the headquarters building. Every parking spot was taken by a Porsche, Lexus, or BMW. All the seats at the only restaurant in the building were taken from 11 a.m. to 8 p.m. with consultants having meetings, planning sessions, or eating lunch with their per diem money. You had to plan your meetings weeks in advance so that you could book a conference room. It got so bad that we had meetings on the front lawn, which eerily reminded me of going to college, when occasionally the professor would conduct class in the quad during a clear spring day. I bet some of the wet-behind-the-ears consults looked longingly out the window at these meetings, reminiscing about being in college just a few months prior.

The money was flowing like a formerly poor, new lottery winner going shopping. Wall Street was throwing money at the company with the thought that it could do no wrong. The company needed to show results; hence the need for the consultants to help speed up the process of integration with the hope of gaining efficiencies (i.e., cutting costs with an eye for increasing the per-share earnings that Wall Street so craved). In the company's eyes, it took money to save money. For the consulting companies, it was like manna from heaven; they could not charge high enough or employ enough bodies.

One particular project with the consultants really sticks out in my mind. The ISP that I was working for had an archaic billing system that at best could be said to have evolved through the years as products were added. It was not robust. It was not that flexible, and it required an army of mainframe programmers to maintain it. It was a relic of the mid-80s that should have been scrapped, but management never wanted to spend the capital if it meant little immediate economic payback. If the capital spent did not boost the share price, the wallet was shut. With the merger, there was a hard look at both companies' billing systems to see which one would prevail. After about three months and countless millions spent on consultants, it was determined that neither company had systems that would require less than $50 million to upgrade fully. Management was approached several times by one of the consultant companies reviewing the current billing systems with information about a generic billing system that the consulting company constructed for other telecom companies. Here was a consulting group supposedly impartially looking at different aspects of the current billing systems, recommending that they scrap them from both companies in favor of a billing system that their company builds.

I knew a couple of the billing people from the ISP who said they could expand the existing billing system to have 90% of the bells and whistles the other systems offered, if they were given a budget of about $10 million. They approached their managers about doing this but were chased away because the managers liked the idea of having a new billing system and a big capital budget.

Upper management asked two consulting companies to bid on creating a new billing system for the company. To do the bid properly, both consulting companies conducted hundreds of hours of interviews with billing, marketing, and customer service to assemble the specifications for the new system. The companies had 120 days to respond, and the winning bid came in just shy of $90 million.

The winner was announced, and upper management signed a three-year contract and allocated $50 million for the first phase of the project. More consultants came. They interviewed more and more billing folks to get their design ideas. They brought dozens of servers into the data center to upload the current data. They looked at the proprietary computer code to see how different parts of the business billed for different services. They copied a lot of the design, the look and feel, and the methodology that the company used to maintain, monitor, and bill its clients on the current billing system. In short, they did almost exactly what the current billing guys suggested but charged a premium for the same solution.

The first phase was due to launch 180 days after the initial contract was signed. There were all types of penalties for not making the delivery date (the ISP was smart in its contracting, at least so far). It took the winning bidder almost 120 days to get anything that somebody could test with up and running on the test servers. In the initial phase, the ISP and the consulting company decided only to roll out billing on three select simple-to-bill products to make sure everything worked as intended. They chose two mass-market products and one corporate product.

Anybody who has worked with computer code knows that it is not always easy to combine existing code without having major or, at least, annoying minor problems. The basic billing engine that the consulting firm used as the basis for the new billing system was solid. It could bill simple Internet products and some data products with some tweaks. The problem was that a lot of the older legacy products were never intended to be billed on this system and required major tweaks to get close to working.

The ISP that I worked for kept changing the specs on what the system needed to do, thus delaying the phase one roll out. This caused the phase one due date to be delayed more than forty-five days along the way. (I am sure that the consulting company was okay with this since it gave them time to tweak their billing system without running out of time with regards to the penalty clauses.) The consulting company did deliver a working system for phase one that handled two simple Internet products, with only a couple of minor glitches that held up billing for only a couple of days. Instead of switching over all existing customers at one time, it decided to do the switch over three billing cycles, where certain portions of the U.S. were cut over to the new system every month. So now the company had three separate billing systems in place: the new one for a couple of Internet products, and two legacy systems in each of the two companies that existed prior to the merger. The ultimate goal was to have one billing system for all products.

The consulting company made the phase one revised due date and received a fair chunk of the money that was contracted to building the billing system (a rumored $50 million). Everyone was encouraged that the new system was in place and the company was able to migrate over existing customers. They started development on phase two of the system roll out. This is where everything fell apart. The consulting company only had experience with billing Internet products and not legacy telecom products. Telecom products tend to be much more complex (think voice minutes, calling features, and hundreds of add-on products). Some products are charged as a monthly fee, some are usage based, and some are both. Imagine all the different promotions and discounts for all the different calling plans, plus the need to have a tax table with over 8,800 different tax jurisdictions in the US. In short, it was a billing nightmare, especially if you have no experience billing that sort of thing. With another deadline looming in the near future and not knowing how to build the billing, they turned to the real experts, the people who were already doing the job at the ISP. These were the same people that management had rejected nine months earlier when they offered to build a cheaper system using the existing platform.

Let's take a step back and look at this from the legacy billing folks' perspective. They were being told that their technology was too old, and more than likely they would either need to be retrained or they would be let go once the new system was in place. These same people were surrounded by overpaid consultants, who were paid almost double what they made, over the last nine months. They were now being mined by the herd of consultants who were hanging on their every word. Every meeting had twenty plus people, with usually ten writing notes at any one time. Instead of designing the system for the consultants, the existing billing team took the stance that they would be professional and answer any questions asked by the consultants accurately, but they would not provide them with any other information. So if the consultants did not ask the right questions, they did not have all the information. This predictably bogged down the design and build process. Every time the consultants uncovered an aspect they missed when designing the solution, they had to go back and recode, retest, and recertify the entire second phase of the billing system. This caused phase two to be delayed numerous times. They missed deadline after deadline. The consultants looked totally incompetent.

Management started to get nervous. They were not seeing the efficiencies they had envisioned when they started the project almost two years prior. In fact, they were seeing the opposite; they had huge consulting bills *plus* they had to keep two complete billing teams on staff to support the legacy systems. This went on for another six months. Phase two was never completed. The consultants could not replace the legacy system completely, so it was never launched. Management decided to fire the consultants working on the new billing system. They wound up having to pay almost the full amount of the contract since the consultants claimed that the ISP kept on changing the specs.

In the end, management wound up giving the legacy billing system guys some more capital, and they were able to deliver a system that combined all the systems over the next twelve months, without any major hiccups. If management had just listened to their own people a layer or two down from the ivory pillar, they would have saved $80 to $90 million, not to mention millions in efficiencies and two years of wasted time. Again, if management had a long-term vision for their company, they would have been designing advanced billing systems all along, knowing that in the future they may need to combine billing systems in the event of them purchasing other companies. Their Short-termitis cost them in the end.

Spending on Marketing Gurus

This is an example of many situations I have experienced, which a lot of readers can easily identify with since most companies have gone through what I am about to describe. This usually takes place when a company is going through a change, or inflection point, and it cannot identify exactly what is happening to the business. The reason it happens at these inflection points is because a business is most interested in either improving the situation that has gone bad or stagnated, or it is experiencing growth that it never planned for and it wants to find out how to control it and harness it.

The tales almost always start like this:

XYZ corporation (if I ever get rich, I want to start a company called XYZ since everyone already talks about it––think of all the money you would save on brand awareness––but I digress) today announces the appointment of Chaz Calvin (fictitious marketing name if there ever was one) as chief marketing officer (CMO).

The employees knew something was up when a bunch of suits descended on the office, squirreling themselves into a conference room, a couple days earlier. All the managers got a chance to meet with the rumored replacement for the last CMO in a two-day "planning" session. Changes were afoot.

Most likely, Chaz is an "old friend" of the CEO (new or old) who appeared to have done a good job for the CEO of another company they both worked at in the past. Chaz is the figment of what a marketing executive should be. He went to a decent school, but not Ivy League. He had some initial success at the past companies that he worked for, which led him to think he is truly better than he really is. We all know a Chaz or two. He tends to wear designer suits, drive a BMW or Porsche (I hereby apologize to these great auto marquis that tend to get lumped in with people like Chaz, with similar personas––pretentious), have a great smile, and typically be either in between marriages or working on his third divorce. In a word: shallow. All show, no go.

Chaz might have come from a bigger competitor or outside the industry; rarely does he come from a smaller company in the same industry. Now he wants to be a big fish in a small pond. Chaz feels that almost everything the company has done prior to him getting there was old and outdated. Chaz knows better than everybody else because he was hired for his experience; at least, he thinks so. In addition, Chaz has a mandate to make changes to how XYZ markets itself.

Not knowing what to do, he buys himself a little time and starts where most CMOs start, spending a lot of money on research and focus groups. He has a need to know the strengths and weaknesses that XYZ has in the end-user's eyes, which is very valid. Most of this information could probably be obtained for free just by speaking to his direct reports and some of the people that report to them. But Chaz does not want to believe what his direct reports tell him about the company's position in the market. He feels that their opinion is incorrect, when most likely they are probably closer to the truth. The reason he feels they are incorrect is because the company is "in trouble," and he is there to play Superman and rescue the company.

The company hires a focus group coordinator to conduct the interviews. Chaz works directly with the focus group company to help create the set of questions about what XYZ is trying to find out. Naturally, his biases come out in the questions. The questions tend to steer the conversations in a direction that matches the conclusions of what his direct reports were trying to tell him. The questions are so poorly written that all they find is what the hotshot intended them to find. Chaz has missed a golden opportunity to find out additional things that can only be found by asking deeper questions. He could have found out things that nobody, including his direct reports, even suspected were happening in the industry. He could possibly have found new ideas for products or solutions. Instead, his controlling nature and general lack of trust in others' abilities, coupled with his insecurities about his position in general, led him to find foregone conclusions.

The focus group report comes back and tells Chaz almost word for word what his direct reports were trying to tell him earlier for free. He takes the costly report and treats it like it is the Holy Grail. He can't wait to show the management team his findings and his solutions to fix the issues. He looks like a genius to management, but in reality he has done a mediocre job at best. He has wasted the company's resources and time getting information that was already known or suspected. In the process, he probably has lost the trust of his staff, which can cause unforeseen and costly long-term circumstances.

Lessons to Learn From This Chapter

There are two separate lessons to learn from this chapter. The first is that if the company truly has a long-term vision, it will build internal systems and processes, processes that include people **and** technical solutions, that can help them grow in the future. The second lesson is that consultants can help, but they should be only brought in **after** the company has tried to find the solution internally (within a reasonable time). Most companies claim they cannot wait and that is why they need to bring in consultants. Take it from someone who has been a consultant for many years––usually the answer, or some of the answer, can be found a couple layers beneath for free. If management is so out of sync to need to hire a consultant to communicate to its own people, then the problem is the management.

Now, I am not trying to ruin the idea of consultancy. Consultants can truly add value if there is a specific situation that the company does not have experience dealing with and it needs to hire some temporary outside help that has the necessary experience. That is, in essence, what a consultant should do. Instead, a lot of managers use consultants as a crutch to support their poor leadership and lack of vision. If managers have developed their people properly over time, they should have a rapport with their employ-ees, and the employees should feel empowered to do what is needed. A lot of managers will claim that I am living in a utopian world wearing rose-colored glasses while sitting in a field of pansies looking for unicorns while preaching from a soapbox. To them I say, "Bugger off and read some man-agement books. Take some classes and learn to do your job well, and then you will get it. Until then, do you want to buy some nice stylish rose-colored glasses, only used on rare occasions from my perch on this lovely soapbox?" Maybe I can sell them on eBay!

CHAPTER 12

Wall Street is Dumb Money

I have a belief that goes counter to what every business school that I am aware of teaches. In fact, I believe it is counter to what most investors and financial people like bankers, stockbrokers, and financial planners think is true. I truly believe that on the whole Wall Street is dumb money. There are people like Jim Rogers, Wilbur Ross, and George Soros who are smart money on an individual basis. I am just saying that Wall Street is dumb on a group basis. In fact, it is so dumb that a lot of time it is the stupidest kid on the entire block, even beating the U.S. and UK governments in the stupid game. But it is not just stupid. It is rich, late, and stupid. The rich and late part is where it gets into serious trouble.

Wall Street prides itself on being early to the party. A lot of people feel that the stock market can predict the direction of the economy six months in advance. It is true that the stock market often moves in the direction where the economy is headed a good six to twelve months in advance. The stock market can also be a faulty indicator because it turns down a lot more than the economy does on the whole. The issue here is that you have talking heads on TV stations like CNBC, Bloomberg, and Fox saying the complete opposite of what is happening, thus confusing most investors. One person might say that this is a bear market rally when in fact it is the start of a long bull market. And just five minutes later, you might get another guest on the same TV station saying that the rally is the beginning of a new bull market.

If you look at what Wall Street is, you get a better understanding why this is so. Wall Street is a place where money migrates looking to make more money. What Wall Street really does is sells things. It sells stocks, bonds, options, and derivatives, but mostly it sells ideas. Ideas and advice are very similar. Some say that advice is nothing more than an educated opinion. In investing, there are only so many ideas that are profitable. The good ideas tend to get crowded fast and eventually they no longer provide such a good opportunity once everyone knows about them. The fact that there is a lot of money chasing a few good ideas leads to herd mentality on a massive scale. Herd mentality is where a lot of individuals all get the same idea about an event and they all proceed in the same direction, similar to a herd of cattle. And, like cattle, this herd does get slaughtered from time to time.

Internet Bubble

I spoke about the Internet bubble briefly when I went over how Worldcom led an industry in thinking that growth rates went to the moon, but Worldcom was not the whole story. From 1995 to 2000, the world was enamored with all things to do with the Internet. The Internet was seen as a great equalizer that would break down the walls of the establishment and allow instant access to information. That did prove to be the case, but nobody ever said that all of the information was good. The information I am referring to was that anybody and anything could be web based.

Entrepreneurs sprang up with all kinds of new websites. Today, many of us cannot imagine a time when you could not go shopping at any time of the day at Amazon.com or bid on your favorite trinket on Ebay.com. These sites, as well as others, were in their infancy. People felt they needed to get in now or all the best ideas would be taken. Wall Street saw the buzz and the amount of money that was being thrown at this new industry and decided they need to be a part of it.

When Wall Street got involved with their deep, dumb money pockets, it was like pouring gas on a bonfire. The bubble was on. If you came to a Wall Street firm during the period from 1996 to 2000 with any stupid idea that was associated with the Internet, you instantly got millions to make your silly site a reality. It got so bad companies were going public (issuing stock on a stock exchange) before they even earned a single dollar. Those in the industry distinctly remember such losers as Pets.com, eToys, and Webvan. All of these were companies that were funded heavily by Wall Street because Wall Street thought they would make a mint selling shares in companies that took an everyday item or service and put it on the web. Many thought the web held vast fortunes because it enabled companies to make their supply stream more efficient, and they could also market to anyone in the world.

The bubble got into such a frenzy that the stock market started attaching outlandish values to many of these companies. I remember a time when Amazon was valued with a total stock market valuation more than Walmart, even though Walmart had over a hundred times more revenue than Amazon. AOL was valued at over $150 billion. It was so large that it was able to take over the mighty Time Warner, a company that had revenue about three times the size of AOL. It was labeled a merger, where AOL shareholders got 55% of the new company even though its revenue and profits were smaller. The total merger at the time was valued at $350 billion. Within a couple of years, AOL Time Warner (the new company name) had to take write-downs for as much as $100 billion some years to erase some of the "goodwill" in AOL's valuation. Finally, in 2009, the two companies separated after destroying hundreds of billions of dollars in the process. At the time, this was the largest bubble, only to be eclipsed by the housing bubble that started two years later in 2001.

The Internet bubble had a knock-on effect of creating side bubbles where companies supplying the Internet companies grew just as fast as the Internet companies. Companies like Cisco, Sun, Juniper Networks, and Corning were all born or reborn during the '90s boom. Their stocks simply exploded. What made these companies different from their customers was that they were actually profitable and had viable business models that are still intact today.

The Housing Bubble

The housing bubble is the perfect example of how "dumb money" Wall Street is. During 2001, the Federal Reserve (Fed) lowered interest rates to (at the time) all-time lows. The Fed lowered these rates to counteract the bursting of the Internet bubble. After the Internet bubble burst, the U.S. economy was in a minor recession. A lot of people felt this was the beginning of a major recession that was finally here to deflate the prices of financial assets that had been in a long super cycle. Stocks, bonds, you name it, were all priced to the moon. The talk of deflation scared the Fed into keeping the rates low for too long. This presented an opportunity for some early innovators on Wall Street to make a lot of money writing new mortgages for U.S. homes.

Unlike in previous recessions, during the recession in 2001, consumers kept on spending. If they did not have the money in the bank, they used credit cards to feed their addiction to shopping. Since interest rates were so low, many people decided to refinance their homes and take money out to pay for their addictive lifestyles (and, in some cases, pay off their charged up credit cards). In addition, the lower rates made people feel that they could pay more for a home because they could now afford a larger mortgage. If you could only afford a payment of $1,000 per month, your $1,000 now went further. Before the drop in rates, it was common to pay 8% or more for a mortgage. At 8%, you could only afford a house worth roughly $170,000 (assuming the regular 20% down at the time). Now, with rates as low as 5.5% for a fixed thirty-year mortgage, you could afford almost a $201,000 house (assuming the same $34,000 down). You could pay 18% more for the house and have the same monthly payment. This caused house prices to explode. As house prices increased, more and more people felt wealthier. They shopped even more. When they could no longer afford their car payments or credit card bills, they simply refinanced their increasingly more "valuable" home and took money out to pay their bills. Wall Street responded to this "need" for money with more money. Wall Street was reaping record profits assembling groups of mortgages into large portfolios and selling them off as bonds backed by the mortgage payments and the ever-increasing value of their homes. Defaults were low because people could always find a buyer for their homes if they got into trouble or needed to refinance.

This led to an explosion of debt. It also led to a self-reinforcing increase in property prices. Some enterprising individuals thought if they owned more than one house that appreciated, they could either refinance them for more cash or simply sell them and make a lot more money one year later. This caused residential (and eventually commercial) property prices to see gains over one year that normally would have taken almost a decade prior to this bubble. Then, in late 2004 and early 2005, people started to take a breather. The sheer number of people with higher credit scores, who previously got mortgages to finance their spending habits during 2001 to 2004, started to run out. Wall Street was addicted to the fees that the mortgages brought. Instead of acting like smart money and raising interest rates because the market got riskier, they did the exact opposite. They started introducing loan programs that had low initial teaser rates that artificially set monthly mortgage payments low for a set period of time before spiking a number of years later. They wrote loans to risky customers with less-than-prime credit histories. They allowed marginal customers to take out loans with lower down payments.

This prolonged the bubble. Prices for homes hit record after record, year after year. Stories of crazy wealth led people to take bigger and bigger risks. People who in the past could barely qualify for a car loan of $10,000 were now getting $200,000 mortgages to purchase houses. This led to lower-end homeowners trading up to nicer neighborhoods using their "equity" from the sale of their homes simply because they owned them for a couple of years and the market price had increased. This led to a mentality where people did not need to worry about whether they could make their mort-gage payments––they just had to take equity out of their ever-increasing home values to make the payments. The dumb money on Wall Street worked overtime looking for ways to feed the bubble. Wall Street even start-ed believing their own hype that "real estate does not go down in value." Similar to what eventually happens to some drug dealers, Wall Street start-ed sampling their own products. Instead of selling the most risky tranches, the parts of the mortgage debt that experience the first hits during a default but also get the highest return, Wall Street kept the risk on their balance sheets or on "off-balance sheet" entities called SIVs. Structured Investment Vehicles (SIV) are separate corporations that were set up by the individual investment banks to "buy" mortgages from themselves so that the banks could take the profits and capital back to write even more loans.

If Wall Street was smart money, this is the time when they should have been running for the exits before the house of cards (pun intended) came crashing down. This did not happen. Wall Street kept defending these loans until it was too late. They were in too deep. And they got stung. So far, Wall Street has received over $2 trillion in equity and loans to try to stop the bleeding. It will probably take at least twice that or more. Does this sound like smart money? To me, it sounds like herd mentality where Wall Street fol-lowed the crowd because they were making money in the short-term. Now they are watching their "equity" go up in flames at rates many more times than the value of the "profits" they made selling the loans. Short-term easy money becomes long-term destruction of value.

A Future Bubble?

I had a hard time labeling this "Future Bubble" because in some aspects this is taking place today. Wall Street has been dabbling in a market many times more bubblicious (if that is a word, not just a great brand of bubble gum) than the Internet and housing bubbles combined. The bubble I, as well as many others, see forming is that of derivatives. Derivatives are financial instruments that "derive" their value from a change in value, price, interest rates, or events of an underlying security. Huh?

A quick example is warranted here to explain them. Say you own an airline and you are worried that the price of gas will increase next month for tickets that you are selling today. You are so worried that if the price increases, the once-profitable ticket will now cost you money. You want to lock in today's gas prices for next month. So you go to an investment bank, and it will sell you a contract to buy one million gallons of Jet A fuel at the current market rate for a transaction fee, but not the actual cost of one million gallons of jet fuel. The investment bank will then turn around and sell that same contract to a jet fuel producer so that the jet fuel producer locks in today's prices for Jet A fuel for next month. Now it knows ahead of time that it will have a buyer at a set rate for a set amount of Jet A fuel. The jet fuel producer pays the investment banker a fee to handle the transaction. The transaction is considered a netted transaction because the investment banker has sold both sides of the contract and has laid off the risk to the individual participants. This is an example of a smart derivative. It serves a purpose, and all parties are happy. The problems come when the banks start speculating.

Let's assume the bank gets a little adventurous and wants to try and make more than the fee it earns for arranging the deal. Staying with the same transaction for one minute, let's assume that one of the bank's economists has made a prediction that Jet A fuel prices will decrease next month. The bank, sensing it can make a profit by reselling a contract at different prices, writes a "covered" contract. A covered contract is one where the amount swapping (i.e., the one million gallons of jet fuel) is covered, but the price points are different. The amount at risk is just the one million gallons multiplied by the spread in price. The bank arranges the deal where it promises to sell the jet fuel to the airline at a set fee of, say, $3.00 per gallon. The bank then goes to the jet fuel supplier and offers to buy the jet fuel at a rate of $2.80 per gallon. The jet fuel supplier speculates it can produce the fuel at a rate lower than $2.80. The bank speculates that it can make $0.20 per gallon times one million gallons plus the transaction fees. The bank makes a little more money for assuming some additional risk.

The problem arises when the bank does not write netted or covered derivatives. It goes with what is called "naked." Naked means that it is assuming all the risk but get all the rewards. Let's assume that the same airline wants to purchase the fuel at $3.00 a gallon for one million gallons. The banks feels sure that the price will decline next month and that it will purchase the jet fuel on the open market at a rate below $3.00 per gallon. Say the bank is right, and jet fuel declines to $2.50 per gallon. The bank makes $500,000 ($0.50 per gallon spread times the one million gallons) plus the transaction fee. This is great for the bank if it gets it right. What happens if it gets it wrong? What happens if gas increases to $3.50 a gallon? Now the bank is sitting on a $500,000 loss (minus the transaction fees). When the bank is naked that means it is exposed to the world, similar to a naked person.

Another risk associated with derivatives is the risk in counter parties. Let's assume that the bank has netted contracts between an airline and a third party, a hedge fund. The hedge fund is taking some risk and it might be naked to earn larger rewards. What happens if that hedge fund has called around and borrowed money to finance its positions? Let's say that the same hedge fund has to pay out more than it has in equity and it goes bankrupt. The bank has a contract between itself and the airline and a separate contract between itself and the now-bankrupt hedge fund. The bank is responsible for meeting the contract with the airline. It thought it was covered but now it is exposed. If you multiply this by thousands of contracts, you can quickly see how this could put a large money center bank out of business, even one that had netted contracts.

The last three examples are easy to value on a bank's balance sheet because you can quantify the exposure based on current market conditions. In banking terms, this is called marked to market. Banks also trade and speculate in contracts that have long-term payouts dates and questionable valuations. These derivatives are not as easy to value as some of the clear-cut examples I gave above. These derivatives are sometimes valued based on models like the Black Scholes model so that banks can show them as an asset or a liability on their balance sheets. In the parlance of the banks, this is called marked to model. In addition, they also use these models as a way of gauging the future profitability of the trade so that the trader can be compensated today. The using of models to gauge profitability is murky at best and leaves a lot of room open to subjective valuation to create the "value" and "profitability" of the transactions. Leaving this much room open with subjective valuations on which to base compensation leads to a lot of gaming of the system. The traders learn quickly how to make a trade appear favorable when in fact the trade may be a future loss maker. It is so murky that traders on both sides of the trade can make the same trade seem profitable to both sides.

Now, step into the shoes of the trader. Let's call him Johnny Green (i.e., the new guy). He is fresh out of business school, and he wants to make a name for himself and retire in the next five years to Turks and Caicos with a few million bucks in the bank. The money center bank puts him on the derivate trading desk to learn the business. At first, all he does is run errands for some of the big-shot traders. He handles some of the paperwork that these big guys hate to do just so he can learn more. They start trusting him more and more. They allow him to place some small covered trades. He makes a small bonus that year. He is disappointed. He starts talking to some of the other traders, and they give him some advice about how they make the big bucks. And then he hears what he has been waiting to hear. An experienced trader tells him a little about how to game the system and do trades that might not settle until three to ten years or more out. That same trader tells Johnny to write (create) contracts in areas that are not heavily traded so valuations are hard to come up with. If he can justify the trade and show how it will be profitable in the future, he stands to make some additional money. What does Johnny care? By the time the position is closed out, he will be retired. He takes some additional risk and is rewarded for it during the bonus time. It encourages him to take on more and more risk, even deploying leverage to make even more money. Before you know it, you have a rogue trader on your hands. Now, in most cases, the risk officer should be monitoring his trading to make sure that the company is not taking on too much risk. The concern with derivates is that the risks are based on models that can be easily gamed.

The models look at individual positions, and positions for the company as a whole. The models take these positions and model the expected outcome and deviations from the outcome based on historic events. The problem with this is that the models, to my knowledge, do not look at systemic risk where a large counter party fails and the weakest link in the chain fails. This is what started to happen when Bear Sterns was taken over in 2008. The Federal Reserve needed to jump in and sell Bear Sterns quickly to JP Morgan to help prevent a meltdown in counter parties.

In my opinion, there is too much risk concentrated in the top four derivative traders, JP Morgan, Goldman Sachs, Bank of America, and Citigroup. Together they control almost 94% of the entire market for derivatives. The notional value of the derivatives that these four companies control is hundreds of times their equity. The notional value is the value of the underlying security that the derivative is based on. It does not mean they own that amount. It simply means they could owe a large change in the notional value of a contract if it goes against them. The average derivative trader has 84% of their trades netted out. Even with that high of a percentage netted, it does not take much to quickly swamp the value of all their equity. Put it another way. The notional value of derivatives worldwide is $55 trillion (with a "T" not a "B"), many times the size of all the equity in all the banks across the entire world, assuming value at risk (VAR) does not exceed 5% of the notional value, or approximately $2.75 trillion. Let's assume that all banks are netted out 84%. That means VAR that is not netted would be roughly $400 billion.

Can the top four banks absorb potentially $375 billion ($400 billion X 94%, which the top four control) in losses after all the ten of billions of dollars they lost in the residential mortgage markets and many more billions soon to be lost in the commercial mortgage market? This would assume 100% loss on their non-netted position, which is highly unlikely but still possible. When you operate with heavily leveraged balance sheets like all four banks do today, it is dangerous to play with leveraged products where asset values could fall precipitously like they did in the RMBS (residential mortgage-backed securities) in late 2008 and early 2009. To make matters worse, a lot of their netted position is netted to leveraged hedge funds, municipalities, and individuals. This is very similar to what happened at AIG, Fannie Mae, and Freddie Mac. Their mortgage (derivatives for AIG) losses were greater than their equity, and the government needed to step in to rescue them in 2008. Fannie and Freddie were reported to be leveraged at over 30:1, meaning they had $30 in debt for every $1 in equity. I do not know AIG's leverage position, but I do not think it was so much leverage due to loans but leverage due to derivative contracts and those contracts moving swiftly against them. A lot of their contracts were netted (probably less than the average), and it only took a couple of weeks before a ninety-year-old company had to be rescued because the financial markets lost confidence that it would remain in business. Wall Street is based on confidence. Once broken, the company either goes out of business or a large entity buys it out at cents on the dollar, or, in the last few years, the government props it up with equity and loans.

When you talk about hundreds of billions of dollars a year in exposure to derivatives that the large money center banks take on, with a large share being speculative, these companies are taking extreme risks. In my opinion when the derivatives bubble bursts, it will make the mortgage crisis of 2007 to 2011 (my guess on the end date) seem trivial. It will most likely take at least one if not all four banks out when it bursts. When 94% of all derivatives are concentrated like this, it just takes one to mess up to take out some or all of the other players, even if those players are netted and financially strong. The numbers are simply too large for any one company **or** country to absorb. To me, the derivative market is the definition of systemic risk. When this happens, these banks will no longer be "too big to fail;" they will be "too big to save." The U.S. government will probably protect the savings accounts (probably only to the FDIC maximum) of the depositors in the companies but let the bondholders, shareholders, and large account holders fend for themselves.

To be fair, Goldman Sachs and JP Morgan appear to be very well-run companies. I have my doubts about Citibank and Bank of America since they have shown their incompetence in the 2008 credit crisis, so it is difficult to say positive things about them. I just think they are not looking at the entire picture of risk that they are taking on. For their sake, I hope the clearinghouse proposal that President Obama and company are working on fixes the derivative market before it blows up. The clearinghouse would standardize a lot of the way that derivatives are written and traded. It would also take away some of the risk because the clearinghouse would absorb some of the default risk. To do that, the clearinghouse would need to have larger resources than the largest player, but it is questionable if that is attainable. This is truly a race against time.

Lesson to Learn From This Chapter

The lesson from this chapter is not to believe the hype about Wall Street. Some individuals are truly smart money, but 95% of Wall Street is dumb money that just happens to have deep pockets and friends. Wall Street is really a selling machine that sells people and companies advice, shares, bonds, derivatives, etc. You must realize that a sales rep is not really truly impartial and that they make money selling things. As such, you should always consider when they are speaking to someone on Wall Street what their motive is, especially when they are dealing with companies that have been known to have fits of massive stupidity in the past.

CHAPTER 13

Hiring New Green Sales Reps to Replace Experienced Older Reps to Save Opex While Destroying Revenues and Relationships

This chapter idea was given to me by a close friend in the telecom industry. Let's call him Robert. Robert is an extremely experienced sales representative of the highest caliber. In the sales world, he is what many would refer to as "The Big Dog" because of the number of large accounts that he lands and the ginormous commission checks he makes. He is so good at what he does that he claims to be able to teach me the ropes so that I can make more money selling than being a consultant. Some days I am tempted. He once told me two separate stories of how different companies he worked for in the UK and U.S. treated experienced sales reps.

The First Story

This story was told to me a long while back by Robert. A company that he worked for in the late '90s and early 2000s did what one of the previous companies I worked for did (as discussed in Chapter 8: Eliminating Customers as a Way to Profitability). The business would flip-flop on the direction that the company would take every eighteen months. During the first cycle, the company would pursue revenue at any cost. It would make deals at break-even profit margins just to inflate the top-line revenue figure to impress the City (British term, for my U.S. readers, referring to the London Stock Market; yes, there are stock markets outside of New York). When the City would tire of valuing businesses on revenue, the company would flip back to pursuing profit margin at any cost.

In 2000, the company that Robert worked for flipped back to pursuing profits (specifically EBITA, which means Earnings Before Interest, Taxes, and Additional Items). To achieve higher EBITA, the company had to do one of two things. It either had to grow profitable new revenue faster or it had to cut costs. Like most companies, it chose the lazy way out, cutting costs. To cut costs, the CEO did a lot of the steps discussed in the CEO 101 chapter. The one thing that strikes me as being out of place is that the management cut the most experienced sales reps because they felt they were paid too much.

In my opinion, sales reps being paid too much is a symptom of a commission scheme that is rewarding the wrong thing. If a company wants to reward profitable growth, it should change the commission plan to incentivize that type of growth––problem solved. Instead, it kept the current commission plan, a plan written when the company was pursuing revenue growth by all means, which did not do what the company wanted. The company was surprised that it did not get the results that it wanted, higher margin customers. Well, duh! What do you expect? Instead of getting the reps to change their focus, the company changed its reps.

The company went and fired at least 50% of its reps, generally its most experienced since they had a higher base salary than newly hired reps. To save a few bucks in salary, the company then hired new sales reps fresh out of college, or wherever sales reps come from these days (don't say under a rock like I know you are tempted to). If you have ever worked in a solution sales environment where it has a little longer sales cycle, you know what I am about to say. Traditionally in telecom, especially since it is heavy solution selling, it takes at least nine months for a sales rep to fill the pipeline if he or she is experienced. For a green sales rep (a term used to describe a brand new sales rep, as in a green tree sapling), it could easily take twelve months or more to fill the pipeline.

As could easily be predicted, after replacing the experienced reps that had full pipelines with brand new green sales reps without anything in the pipeline, new sales came to a screeching halt. Instead of improving margins over the next few quarters, margins shrank. They shrank because the normal churn in older customers, who tended to pay more because of the nature of a deflationary industry like telecom, were not replaced with any new customers, or at least not at the same pace. The green reps started trying to fill their pipelines, but sales cycle length was working against them. Coupled with the base salaries that the company had to pay the new sales reps, the equation was going in the wrong direction.

Within six months, management realized they made a great mistake and started to fire the new green sales reps, which were just now just starting to fill their pipelines. To fix this lack of production by the new sales reps, management started trying to hire experienced sales reps from other companies. They offered to pay higher-than-industry-standard base salaries and commissions. They went on a hiring binge. The problem here is that these experienced reps had to build a new pipeline of customers because a lot of them had contracts that forbade them from poaching their existing customers. At least they were able to start filling their pipelines with customers within six months.

The silly thing about this situation is as soon as the company started hiring experienced reps to get accounts with large margins, it did its eighteen-month flip-flop and decided to concentrate on revenue. The City was now looking for top-line revenue growth instead of margin growth. The company now had to now start having the sales reps concentrate on bringing in new business that was higher revenue regardless of the cost. That means the reps had to start looking at different customers to fill their pipelines. All these stop-start situations led to mass confusion and a stagnating company. Instead of playing their own game, the company was playing the City's game and they were losing badly.

The Second Story

This next story is humorous and sad at the same time. It is humorous that it happened but tellingly sad about the lack of management that the company had. It all started in 2001. A company that I worked for in the U.S. hired a new sales rep at about the same time I started as a senior manager for pricing. This is when I met Robert. Robert had once worked for a large company that had an excellent sales training program. It taught him technical selling skills as well as incredible people skills. Unlike most sales reps, he was almost understated. He was not showy or flashy; he was very amiable and a little on the techno geeky side. Most people thought that they were getting the better of him because he was so amiable and easygoing. These traits led a lot of customers to instantly like him.

He could talk to the chief technology officers (CTO) in their language as well as talk financial to the chief financial officers (CFO) at some of the world's largest companies. He became so well liked that a lot of the companies would not make a move on their worldwide Internet and data networks without his input. Talk about being in a powerful position. All he had to do was fill out the orders, and he would easily make $300K to $400K a year. What made this even more remarkable is that he had the largest sales pipeline in the company within six months of starting with the company.

His sales records year after year made everyone in the company look like a "goddamn genius" (to steal a phrase from the movie *Forrest Gump*). His bosses were quickly promoted to division managers (chief operating officers, or COOs) and CEOs of sister companies hoping that their "management wisdom" would help out those divisions and sister companies. Some of his senior vice presidents of sales (SVP) were hired away to work at competitors at double their current salaries. People who worked closely with the department that Robert worked in knew that most of the results were from him and very little were from his peers. After about four years, Robert got tired of doing the sales thing and wanted to move into management. He felt that he could do a better job training the sales team to be as good as he was if not better. After his most recent SVP of sales left, he applied for the role and was turned down. He was turned down not because of his results, but because his results were too good and the company did not want him distracted with management responsibilities. The company wanted him selling full time so that it made its bonuses. To make matters worse, it promoted the second best sales rep (above-average but not as good by a mile as Robert). His name was Peter.

Peter was a typical sales rep. He was slick and could handle customer objections with relative ease. Like Robert, he too was a career sales rep. Unlike Robert, he felt sales was something you were born with and could not be taught––either you had it or you didn't. To top it off, Peter was all about Peter looking good, not about the company or the people under him looking good. If it benefited Peter, it was done; if it did not, it rarely got done.

Peter was a little jealous of Robert and the money that Robert earned. He was also jealous of the constant praise Robert received from the company and the higher management. Peter felt that Robert was lucky and that a lot of the sales that Robert made were from being in the right place at the right time and having the right accounts on his list. Peter did not see that a lot of Robert's list was made up from relationships that Robert created and fostered to great success. Robert was not handed these large accounts; he earned them.

When it came time to go over the new sales commissions plan for the following year, Peter purposely stuck it to Robert. He did not want Robert to earn more than him. To do this and seem to be fair and not appear to be going after Robert, Peter raised the minimum sales commission levels that all the reps had to achieve to get 100% of their bonuses. By raising the bar and not spending any time training the other sales reps, a number of mediocre reps became poor reps in the eyes of the company. Not only did they not achieve full commission like they once did, a number of them were reprimanded and given warnings that if they did not improve, they would be fired. This caused a bunch of these okay reps to decide to leave the company. Robert just worked harder and exceeded his targets and made larger bonuses.

Peter's ego could not handle Robert making more than him, so he started to ride Robert extra hard. Peter scrutinized all of Robert's client expenses (lunches, bar tabs, etc.). He also created a multi-tiered sales commission scheme that pretty much singled out Robert by himself at the top of the scheme. The new commission scheme raised Robert's base salary but doubled his quarterly quota. It had a larger bonus scheme but capped his earnings at a lower amount than what he was able to earn in a couple of really productive sales quarters in the past. Peter felt that Robert would not make his quota or, at best, he would barely make it and his commissions would be a lot less.

In addition to Peter trying to lower Robert's commission, Peter had some ethical issues that Robert did not like. Peter would promise things to customers and to Robert and then go back on his promises. Peter would also delegate some of his tasks to Robert so that Peter could have more time to "manage" the rest of the team. These tasks took Robert away from selling a good 30% of the time. Combining the decreased time for selling and the almost impossible commissions plan, Peter finally succeeded in lowering Robert's commissions so that he earned less than what Peter made.

By this time, Robert had become known in parts of the telecom industry. A lot of the old SVPs who had gone on to become CEOs and COOs at other companies were itching to get Robert to jump ship and come work for them. For the year prior to when Peter took over, Robert had rejected numerous offers just because he was comfortable working at the existing company. Robert just wanted to earn a decent living so that he could spend quality time with his family and friends, and have enough money to put away for a comfortable retirement in hopefully five to ten years. He knew he could make more money somewhere else, but he felt a loyalty to the company that he had helped grow dramatically. He wanted to see the company succeed.

After Peter took over and made the changes to the commission scheme, Robert felt less and less loyal to the company that was, in essence, screwing him. He seriously started looking at the offers from the competitors. Then one day his old boss from a couple years prior was promoted to CEO of a different company. His old boss offered him a base salary that was twice as much as his current base salary. In addition, he offered him a higher percentage of total sales without a cap. On truly remarkable quarters where his productivity was high, he could potentially earn $500K+. For Robert, this was a no-brainer. He gave his notice. The CEO of the existing company made a lot of last-minute offers to try to keep him, but ultimately Robert wanted to get away from working for Peter, and Peter was staying. The decision was made, and Robert tried to give two months' notice. The company wound up taking only two weeks and then dismissed him early.

The value of Robert became apparent after he left. The company continued to make its forecast of new revenue for the next five quarters based largely on the deals that Robert made. One of the existing sales reps that Robert mentored started stepping up and took over Robert's role as "The Big Dog." After five quarters and poor leadership in sales management, the pipeline started to run dry. Peter panicked and started looking around for jobs in other divisions and other companies so that he could leave on a positive note. I left the company shortly after. I have not heard from Peter, but I assume that he has gone on to other endeavors (the politically correct term meaning he was forced out, which I am purely speculating). As for Robert, he took an active SVP of sales role. He tells me that he only sells about 50% of the time, and he manages other salespeople the rest of the time. If I know Robert, and I know him well, I bet every one of those sales reps will be a star, and I bet he would not mind one bit if they **all** earned more than he did. To Robert, that would be a sign of success and not failure like it was for Peter.

Lack of Sales Training

There are a lot of companies that have the same misconceptions about sales as Peter did. A lot of companies feel that the ability to sell is something ingrained and cannot be taught. This is totally false. Additionally, some companies skimp on sales training as a way to "save" money. Notice how I put save in quotes. To me, this is one of the most expensive things a company can do; it is almost as bad as cutting back on advertising. Let's discuss these two misconceptions in more detail to help dispel these myths that I am seeing more and more, especially in the U.S.

Sales is taught **and** seems ingrained (for some). I know it sounds like I am talking out both sides of my mouth (I am a consultant, after all), but I am doing it for a reason. Some people seem to have been selling since they were just learning to walk, and they were. These people who are natural sales reps learned to sell to their parents, grandparents, teachers, or just fill in the blank with whoever they were in contact with. These persons learned to sell to their audience to get what they wanted or get their way. They learned from an early age how to sell. They might not have taken a course, but they did learn it. Instead of taking a course or reading a book, they learned from reading their environments. To my knowledge, they have yet to discover a gene or sequence of genes that can be associated with having the ability to sell.

The fact that there is a multibillion-dollar sales training industry dedicated to teaching people the art and science of selling means that there must be a way to be taught to sell. Just think of all the money that is spent annually for all the seminars, CDs, books, online courses, just to improve someone's sales techniques. There are famous companies dedicated to sales training. Think of Dale Carnegie, Zig Ziglar, and Anthony Robbins, just to name a few. I am not in sales, but I have taken sales classes in college. I have bought tapes and read books on the subject just to help my professional career, not because I wanted to be a sales rep, but because I recognize the value that they can teach me in handling clients, contracts, and just plain dealing with people. One of the biggest things you get from learning to sell is the ability to deal with difficult people and to get them to see your point of view. In my opinion, everyone who has a job working with people could benefit from taking a sales course or reading a sales training book.

Robert was fortunate enough to have worked for a company when he first started that believed in heavy sales training. The company was an S&P 500 company that required him to attend four weeks of sales training (and pass multiple sales tests along the way) before he was allowed to move to the next level. The four weeks of sales training taught him the basics of selling, handling rejects, cold calling, presentations, and creating a customer target list. He had to learn that before he was allowed to work with an experienced sales rep. Once he was through the four-week training course, he spent another six months working under an experienced sales rep to learn his territory, his products, and the way the company expected him to do things. It may sound like a long, drawn-out process that would be time consuming and expensive for the company to undertake. The company felt it made its sales reps the best in the industry; hence, they were more productive and they had more revenue and higher margins as a result.

Let's look at it another way. In most industries with higher ticket items or services, it generally takes sales reps, on average, up to twelve months before they meet their quotas on a consistent basis. If you can shorten that by a month or two, think of the additional revenue the company can make. Plus, think of the money that it saves. Most companies pay a base salary in addition to a sales commission. Here is a quick comparison of a rep with training and a rep without training.

For this example, we will assume that the sales reps for two separate companies make a base salary of $40K per annum. They sell a service with a monthly fee (not a one-time sell). They are expected to close $1 million in new business per year ($83K in annual new business per month). The rep with sales training is assumed to be 25% more productive. Sales training costs are $5,000 for the four-week course. Typically, I have seen that a trained rep is productive by his or her ninth month in the field, while an untrained rep on average takes more than twelve months to meet his or her quota (we will use month twelve as the quota being met).

Annual Base Salary	$40,000			Annual Base Salary	$40,000		
Commission	10%			Commission	10%		
				Productivity Difference	25%		

Sales Month	Untrained Rep			Trained Rep			
	Salary	Sales	Commission	Salary	Sales	Commission	Difference
Month 1	$3,333	$2,000	$200	$3,333	In Training	$0	-$2,000
Month 2	$3,333	$5,000	$500	$3,333	$2,500	$250	-$2,500
Month 3	$3,333	$10,000	$1,000	$3,333	$6,250	$625	-$3,750
Month 4	$3,333	$20,000	$2,000	$3,333	$12,500	$1,250	-$7,500
Month 5	$3,333	$30,000	$3,000	$3,333	$25,000	$2,500	-$5,000
Month 6	$3,333	$40,000	$4,000	$3,333	$37,500	$3,750	-$2,500
Month 7	$3,333	$50,000	$5,000	$3,333	$50,000	$5,000	$0
Month 8	$3,333	$60,000	$6,000	$3,333	$62,500	$6,250	$2,500
Month 9	$3,333	$70,000	$7,000	$3,333	$83,000	$8,300	$13,000
Month 10	$3,333	$75,000	$7,500	$3,333	$103,750	$10,375	$28,750
Month 11	$3,333	$80,000	$8,000	$3,333	$103,750	$10,375	$23,750
Month 12	$3,333	$83,000	$8,300	$3,333	$103,750	$10,375	$20,750

Total Salary & Commission	$92,500		Total Salary & Commission	$99,050
Total Sales	$525,000		Total Sales	$590,500
Cost of Sales	18%		Cost of Sales	17%

Sales Difference Because of Training	$65,500
Cost of Training	$5,000
Additional Commissions	$6,550
Net Benefit to the Company	**$53,950**

You can see from the table on the previous page that, starting in the seventh month, the trained sales rep catches the untrained rep and then proceeds to leave him or her behind. The benefits to the company are many. First, it gets higher revenue, and revenue increases faster. Second, it has a more productive sales team and presumably a more satisfied group of employees, which will incur lower employee turnover. Third, the company's cost of sale is lower since it gets higher sales for the same base salary. The $5,000 spent initially pays for itself by the end of the eighth month. Obviously, the company that spends its money to do an initial training is more apt to spend money on repeated sales training; thus, there is additional training cost through the year. Like the old saying goes "If you think education costs a lot, try ignorance." Can you tell my wife's a teacher?

Lesson to Learn From This Chapter

The lesson to learn from this chapter is a simple one. Successful people rise to the top. Their value in terms of dollars is not always as easy to identify as Robert's (direct sales is easy to measure). These superstars have the ability to change an organization just by their work ethic. Just like putting Peyton Manning or Sidney Crosby into a lineup, they change the dimension of the game. Suddenly average players look like superstars just because they lift their game in relation to the star players out of respect and duty and not out of fear. You cannot put a dollar figure on a true team-playing superstar versus somebody who is playing for his or her own notoriety. The person who is just doing it for the notoriety might be a great player, but will never become legendary in business or sports, like a superstar team player.

In addition to superstars, a company needs a well-trained sales team. It needs day-to-day players who can produce consistent results. The more they know about selling and how to handle situations that arise (either by learning through experience or training), the more productive they will be.

CHAPTER 14

Business Self-help Books Pointing Out the Ways of Industry Leaders: Your Guide for Which Stocks to Short Sell Within the Next 24 Months

I once worked for a company that appeared as a business case in a book in the mid-1990s. The company was put up on a pedestal by this book as the leader in customer service in the telecommunications industry. I was actually working in the customer service department supporting large customers during the time when the book was written and appeared briefly in the bookstores. Stroking my own ego a bit, I would personally like to think I played a major part in getting that esteemed recognition due my own diligent pursuit of making our customers exceedingly pleased, but, alas, It was probably not me who made the difference.

Working in that call center, I was one of maybe 250 employees all supporting a midsized company that specialized in business telecommunications. Most of the people were fresh out of college. Many would come in hungover first thing in the morning from being out until 2 a.m. or later the night before. The job was really easy. I got so bored in my position that I played twenty questions with every customer calling in, just to see if I could solve their issue within twenty questions. I also figured out that if I went to work right away first thing in the morning, bright and early at 8 a.m., I got a bunch of easy calls where people's phone lines were out of service from something that might have happened after hours. Most of the call center people were too busy trying to nurse their hangovers from the night before by drinking copious amounts of caffeine in any delivery mechanism available. The ways to fix the callers' issues were so easy, and it usually only took a couple of minutes of troubleshooting to figure out a resolution. A person could rack up tons of calls in a short period of time. We were required to take sixty-four calls per day (average eight calls per hour, for those playing along on the home version). I would routinely get my quota by 11 a.m., and then I could slack with my friends and still get over a hundred calls answered. I looked like a superstar with only four hours' worth of actual work being done. I think this is why I eventually became a consultant.

The call center felt like I was still in college. There was always a party at someone's house after work or at the nearest pub. People always seemed to take a smoke or coffee break ten minutes before the hour, similar to when classes typically let out.

Do the previous paragraphs sound like the making of "Best Customer Service in the Telecommunications Industry?" I seriously think not! If we were the best at that time with the number of screw-ups who were employed, I would hate to see the worst customer service! Images of calling the worst customer service, where you are put on endless hold or forced to talk to somebody for whom English is not their first language, come to mind. God help the people who have to toil there to earn a few bucks.

I seriously think we got nominated for one of two reasons. The first is that, at the time, when you called the toll-free number for support, a live person answered the phone. That is a rarity even today. The back story was, I think, that management was too cheap to spend the money on a proper IVR (Interactive Voice Response; the annoying devices that ask you to hit one to speak to a sane person). I guess sometimes being cheap and clinging to old ways can seem charming to some. That is probably how Cracker Barrel makes so much money even though it tries to be country in a Disney-ish way, next to major interstates in the U.S. The second reason I think we got nominated was that we were large enough that we had a name in our industry, but very few people could dispute that we were good or bad. Unless you were the telecom's manager for a company or you had problems making a phone call, you simply did not have any good or bad experiences to dispute the author's claim. Simply put, the company had a name that was associated with a growing company in a high-tech industry where few would ever try their customer service. The author borrowed the company's reputation, willingly given by the management, to complete a book that allowed him to make a few bucks. As you will see, we authors tend to do that a lot. I am throwing my name in this bunch after the shameful ass kissing I did in chapter ten where I talked at length about four CEOs/famous investors.

The Madden Curse

The Madden Curse is a reference to John Madden, a former NFL player and present Hall of Famer, who has a popular video game called *Madden (and the year when it comes out)*. The game is eagerly awaited by gamers in North America every year when it debuts in September to coincide with the beginning of the NFL football season. John Madden or EA Sports, the game's developer, picks out who will have the honor of being the football player on the cover of the game case. When it was first done in 1999, it was initially seen as such a great honor that players were pushing their agents to get them on the cover so that they would forever be immortalized. Starting in 2004, some players became apprehensive about being on the cover. The reason stems from the fact that a perceived curse befalls the player within a couple of years of appearing on the cover, usually in the same season. There has been a coincidence where a number of cover "winners" have had season-ending injuries or off-field incidents that have harmed their careers or reputations to one degree or another. Whether this is a curse or not, I do not know. One has to wonder if it is simply dumb luck in a game that is violent, with the threat of injury that is always present, or if there is something more to it. I will get out my voodoo dolls now to protect myself.

Businesses have a similar curse. Whenever a business starts to stand out, an author or multiple authors race to be the first to showcase the company as a world-beater. The authors want to stand out by borrowing the company's name to sell books to make money. They may have some other higher calling about wanting to improve the way business is done or some other type of BS, but mostly it is done to sell books so that the author can eat. Starving authors and artists can be so fiendish.

I started noticing that whenever a company gets too big for its own britches, these books start popping out of the woodwork (actually, the printing presses). These books usually go through some type of grandiose history of the company where the founder initially banged away in the garage to create some world-class company making software or something high tech (lately), or a new invention the world suddenly needed (in the past). Why do you need to work in a garage if you are writing software or doing something high tech, I do not know, but it just seems like the founder is always stuck working in the garage. Maybe he and the missus do not get along so much now that he is always tinkering and trying to get rich, and it forces him to seek solitude, but I digress. The author then goes through the struggles in the early years and how, if the moon and the stars did not align just right early on, the company would have failed. Ooh, drama! My spine tingles at the thought––if we never had an eBay or Enron, where would the world be? I think they do that for effect or the authors try to put in a secret romantic spin that keeps readers reading and their books selling. After the company emerges through its teenage years, it starts becoming the company that everyone wants to beat. Its growth goes absolutely parabolic. The company looks as though, if nobody stops it, it will produce enough revenue to match the GDP of a small South American country in a matter of a few short years.

The general public notices something is different. They claim the company must be doing something unique. We need to analyze them and find the secret to their success. Since many authors have never worked outside of writing, they do not know much about business. They assume that successful companies must have a magical feature or function that separates them from the rest. They equate incredible growth rates with success. They come to believe the hype. They write their books to make the company and their leaders look mythical, surreal. They quickly claim that if other companies do not adopt such measures as the company is using pronto, they might as well not show up on Monday morning because there will be no business left.

The leaders and some of the higher-up employees at the companies held on the proverbial pedestal start walking around like they are God's gift to business. Their chests swell as well as their heads, along with their stock value. They start to believe their own press. And this is where most of these revered companies start to stumble. They look to expand even more. They press into new areas of business. They look at taking out competitors as a way to seek domination in their industries. I would hazard a guess that their leaders start getting served more papers for divorce from their wives or husbands because they can no longer live with their oversized egos and thoughts of self-importance.

As time goes by, usually twelve to eighteen months, it all starts to unravel. No longer are they growing as fast. Their market share gets stagnant. Less and less is written about their brilliance. Their stock price slips slightly, under the guise of profit-taking from the huge run-up over the last few years.

I have noticed this pattern time and time again. I started noticing it in the late '90s when companies like AOL, eBay, Worldcom, Yahoo!, and Enron were treated like celebrities that could do no wrong. More and more books came out saying these were the companies of the future and the world was changing. The books would claim that they revolutionized their industries and how business was done in general. Their leaders would be keynote speakers at conventions. Some would go so far as to write books about their own clever management ways. People would throw money at them like it was confetti. As some would say, this was the "period of maximum stupidity." I tend to agree.

Instead of getting fed up with the BS, I learned to step back and look at this as an opportunity. In the pattern that I noticed, usually about twenty-four to thirty-six months after the books and articles come out claiming their brilliance, there would be a major correction in perception about the company. With the change in reputation came a giant swoon in their stock prices. It was so consistent that you could almost set your watch by it. If I were so bold, I would look to buy PUTS, which are an option on a stock that allows you the right to sell a stock at a higher price in the future. This is similar to selling a stock short without the potential for catastrophic loss; only the cost of the PUTS themselves is at risk. I made a little money doing this to the U.S. homebuilders as well as a couple of banks in 2006 and 2007. I chickened out and sold them too early. That is another story.

Today I am seeing stories about Apple, Google, Research in Motion, JP Morgan, and Goldman Sachs (the last two stumbled, but they are now more revered because of how they made it through the financial crisis of 2007-09). All five companies are great companies, but I would wager that at least three of the five will experience a serious fall in stock price and reputation by the middle of 2013. The three that experience a hiccup will likely see their stock prices drop by 50% to 90%; some might even fail or have to be bought out. I would hazard some guesses on which ones it would be, but I would purely be speculating without an ounce of knowledge or insight. I am just mentioning the pattern and the psychological reasons behind the drop, not the business reason. Short or buy PUTs at your own risk.

I did notice the new book about Jamie Dimon that just hit the bookstores in April 2009, and smiled a knowing smile. Some author has put the CEO of JP Morgan Chase on a pedestal to be admired for his handling of the credit crisis in 2007 to 2009. In my opinion, it is probably too early to say we have emerged from the crisis since we have yet to experience stable growth. I have not read the book, but I suspect that it says something to the effect that Jamie kisses babies everywhere he goes and that he has special blue undershirts with a large "S" on them. If I were Jamie, I would be like some of the NFL players who are shunning being on the cover of the latest Madden video game out of fear of injury or having an off-field incident damage their reputations. He should try his best to avoid the "business book writer's curse," which could be equally damaging to his wallet. Jamie, consider yourself warned.

Example to Check in October 2011

In October 2009, a book came out called *Blackberry Planet: The Story of Research in Motion and the Little Device that Took the World by Storm* by Alastair Sweeney. It is a well written book that takes a relatively boring subject of a business's history and makes it exciting and motivating for the reader. You can't help but want to cheer on RIM and their Blackberry device when you are through with the book. The author expresses the predictable touts and praises how the company has taken the world by storm and that it is the best thing since sliced bread. Research in Motion (RIM) truly came out with a device that changed mobile telephones. Before the Blackberry, a person had to go out and download their mail to their device. With RIM's breakthrough, the device is automatically updated with the latest email in what seems like less than a second. Sometimes it actually beats the email over my corporate LAN! To the author's defense, he has a final chapter entitled *Rim on the Plateau?* Mr. Sweeney does point out some weaknesses in RIM's products and business model especially when compared to Apple's iPhone.

The point I am trying to make here is that authors latch on to hot topics all the time just to sell books. Whenever a company gets so universally known and accepted as being the best, inevitably it is starting its downfall. I am speculating that by October 2012, RIM's stock will have lost at least 50% to 90% of its value purely because it is getting too big for its britches. This is sort of an easy prediction because it is already starting to see slowing growth in sales of its devices in late 2009. The company thinks it is due to the worldwide recession. My opinion is that most people who already wanted a Blackberry have purchased one, and people are moving on to trendier products like Apple's iPhone. The marginal buyers' indifference to the device will eventually lead the Blackberry device to go the way of Palm's Treo and Motorola's RAZR phones, all once extremely popular mobile phones replaced with newer trendier phones. On October 6, 2009, RIM's stock (symbol RIMM) closed at $66.43 on the NASDAQ. I am speculating (**read: do not** invest unless you do your own research—I take no responsibility for my own bonehead prediction. In fact, I am not even stupid enough to be putting my own money on the line, and neither should you) that the stock will be worth between $33.22 to $6.65 per share by Friday, October 5, 2012. Please remember that I am a silly author, not a professional investor, and I am speculating that a price will decline based solely on what another author is touting as the latest "best" company or product. This should never be the basis of a decision on purchasing or selling short a stock. Only time will tell if my theory will hold water or if I am full of crap.

Lesson to Learn From This Chapter

The lesson from this chapter is that once your business is successful, do not let it go to your head. Just because some hack of a writer is trying to make a quick buck on the flavor of the day and needs a subject to write about, do not assume what he prints is correct. It will be somewhat accurate, but chances are it will not be correct. Yes, you are probably doing something different. You might have a unique product or service. You might even have the most dominating market share in the history of your industry. You might have even figured out a way to manage a company that truly sets your firm apart from others. This is usually when it all blows up in your face. You get cocky. You start believing your own success. You then start making mistakes or start taking it easy.

Your competitors start copying what you are doing or what you are making. At first, it seems a little annoying, but it typically is the seed of the thing that brings you down a notch. If you notice what Microsoft does, you will know what needs to be done. You need to buy out your smaller competitors that have a competing technology to either squash it or adapt it to your product or service. This is similar to all the mafia movies where their own people get them in the end.

CHAPTER 15

Over-leveraged

Like many readers, as especially the ones in the U.S. and UK will attest, we all got a little carried away over the last decade. We as individuals, companies, and governments decided that if we did not buy something now that it would be too expensive in the future. Since 2000, the U.S. government has reported that Consumer Price Index (CPI) has averaged 2.5% per year. Most people equate the CPI with inflation. In reality, all it measures is a basket of "goods and services" that the U.S. government interprets to represent what an average American purchases. Starting in the mid-1990s, the economists at the Bureau of Labor Statistics (BLS) started to play with the basket of goods by introducing a quality bias to the measure. They also introduced another change to the index by calculating a "rental equivalent" measure to allow economists to compare the cost of homeownership versus renting a property. The quality bias was designed to take into consideration that products and services improve over time, and it can show up in the price of products and services but might not really be inflationary. Perfect example is the automobile. If you compare a car built in 1991 to one built in 2011, there is a night and day difference. The 2011 model more than likely has antilock brakes, air bags, better gas mileage, improved safety, etc. The BLS tries to adjust prices over time to compensate for the improvements in the products. The rental equivalent change tries to adjust the cost of homeownership so that it can be measured in the inflation number. As you can imagine, anything the government does over time grows into an unruly mess, and so do these measures. Since 2001, some have felt that these two different changes could have lowered the official measure of inflation in the U.S. by almost 3% annually. People who purchased a property or a vehicle know the price they paid has increased dramatically since 2001.

To help get out of the recession in the U.S. in 2001, the Federal Reserve reduced key interest rates to 1% in an effort to stimulate the economy into recovery. With lower interest rates came a refinancing boom that allowed consumers to withdraw equity from their homes while maintaining monthly mortgage payments at nearly the same monthly fees as their old payments. The amount owed increased, but because interest rates had plummeted to rates not seen in a generation, they caused the mortgage payment to either decline, stay the same, or increase slightly depending on the amount of the increase in the loan. In addition to the refinance boom, a lot of buyers found out that they could purchase bigger homes with larger mortgages for the prices that they were paying today for their mortgages on their old houses. This led to an increase in demand for higher priced homes. The increase in house prices fed an additional increase in demand for homes for three reasons. The first reason for the increased demand was that homebuyers felt that if they did not purchase houses soon, the prices would be too high for them to ever purchase homes of their own. This increased the supply of buyers. The second way this increase in prices fed on itself was that now people had increased equity in their current properties from the increasing home prices, which, coupled with the reduced interest rates, allowed them to purchase even more expensive homes. Finally, Wall Street, being the dumb money that it is, was late as usual with pockets of cash to throw at the newly forming bubble. It saw the increase in demand for money and decided that it wanted to play a bigger role in this growing market. Greed led Wall Street to continue the boom far longer than it should have naturally lasted by offering even cheaper money in the form of Alt-A and interest-only loans to weaker and weaker borrowers. This money sprinkled on weak buyers was like a fat person salivating at an all-you-can-eat buffet. They could not stop themselves, and the housing bubble grew to extraordinary levels of leverage (debt) by both borrowers and Wall Street. This happened until, like all bubbles, it popped. And this is what led to the credit crisis from 2007 to 2009 (and most likely longer).

Like consumers and investment banks, investors, companies, and governments sometimes lose their better judgment when it comes to taking on leverage. They sometimes get lost in their ways and listen to Wall Street blindly. At first, Wall Street offers companies the ability to sell bonds to help them finance long-term investments. If the cost of capital is below the return on the long-term investment, it usually makes sense for a company to borrow the money instead of using internally generated funds to cover the cost of the investment. The company does the analysis and says it can either do one project or another with internal funds, or it can do both projects if it borrows the money. Wanting to improve its results for the shareholders, it takes on both projects to boost the overall results of the company, i.e., it leverages its balance sheet to be able to do both projects. Doing both projects in theory should boost results of the bottom line, which should loosely translate into a higher stock price. If a CEO has a good year as a result of doing both projects, you can bet that his or her board is begging to do it again.

Wall Street has another solution for what the company can do with the money it raised in the bond offering. Since most publicly listed companies reward their top employees with stock options, Wall Street convinces the company management to try something else that might benefit the company's shares and possibly lift the value of its options. Their idea is that the company should use the money to buy back some of its shares on the stock market. Wall Street sells this to the CEO and the board as a way to improve their earnings per share (EPS); their reasoning is simple. If you maintain the same profits but put them over fewer shares, your EPS increases. This also could potentially increase the value of the shares because there are fewer shares and greater earnings (per share). If the stock moves higher, the board gets addicted to it. Next thing, the board is announcing to the public about a new large share buyback authorization.

Soon the company is addicted to raising more and more debt. Every project, every buyback has the potential to boost the share price. The addiction spreads, and Wall Street has another addict in need of a fix. The company starts looking at other ways to "enhance shareholder value," a nice and friendly term that usually implies either leveraging the crap out of the balance sheet or making dramatic changes to the company either through share buybacks or a merger with another company, or through selling the businesses, or spinning off divisions—all items designed to boost the share price in the short term typically with little thought of the long-term implications. The company decides that it is cheaper to buy out its competitors using debt than it is to try to beat them one on one. On paper, it is cheaper—until the integration takes place. It usually takes a couple of years before the real price tag is known. The animosity between integrating companies is revealed usually in the poor results of the integrated company that is not truly integrated. The integration has a bunch of invisible costs, like incompatible systems, that take millions of dollars to make work together, and disgruntled employees who do not want to go beyond their normal jobs to make the merger work. At the same time, it still costs a lot to finance the company debt. The company soon becomes trapped.

The Wrong Time to Lever Up

In investing, timing is everything. Buy what you think is the right stock at the wrong time, and you can lose a lot of money. Buy a poor stock at the right time, and you can make a lot of money. The same thing can happen for a business intent on expanding by purchasing a competitor or adding a new line of business. If it misses the business cycle, its hard work can be for naught. A similar thing can also happen if a company takes on leverage at the wrong point of the business cycle. Combining the two can be suicidal to most businesses. As easy money flows and perceived risk diminishes, businesses get more adventurous and look to do "transformational" deals. "Transformational deal" should be the synonym for large, stupid, and ill-timed. Usually the company is gambling on its future, and more than likely it is directly tied to the bravado of the CEO or president.

History is littered with deals that, in hindsight, should never have been made. Think about deals like AOL's purchase of Time Warner, Mercedes Benz's purchase of Chrysler, Citigroup's purchase of Travelers Group, and AT&T's purchase of TCI (a large cable company). These deals were done at or near the peak of the market cycle, using a method of finance that was also peaking (debt or shares, depending on the business cycle). All the boards promoted the deals as one plus one equaling more than two (i.e., large synergies for combining the two entities). They were all considered transformational at the time. The only thing they transformed was taking two companies and making them worth less together than they were individually before the deal was done. None of the companies mentioned stayed together more than ten years before their marriages ended in bitter divorce.

Macklowe

From 2003 to 2007, commercial real estate in the U.S. (as well as Europe) exploded. Prices increased regularly by double digits for both purchase and rent. The increase in value and lowered interest rates caused a boom in a lot of geographic areas in construction of commercial properties. Still, in some areas that had limited space available for construction or where demand for space was extremely high, it led to property owners demanding higher and higher prices for both sales and rents. Property investors purchased property with the anticipation that values and rents would continue to increase. That, combined with the easy money from Wall Street via commercial mort-gage-backed securities (CMBS) led to a property bubble. One of the famous property investors that got caught in this mess was Macklowe Properties.

Harry Macklowe got started investing in New York real estate in the mid-1960s. Macklowe Properties is known as a big developer in the Manhattan real estate market. It has developed, managed, or owned up to seventeen million square feet of commercial real estate and over three thousand residential units. Most of the properties that Macklowe Properties own are considered class "A" or "A+ trophy" buildings, which are considered the absolute best properties in terms of value and rents. To grow a company from literally nothing to a giant colossus in a little over forty years by strictly investing and developing real estate in the New York market says a lot about what Harry and his sons have accomplished. You do not get to the size of Macklowe Properties by not knowing what you are doing.

In 2003, Macklowe purchased the two-million-square-foot GM building from Donald Trump and Conseco Insurance for $1.45 billion. Macklowe only used $50 million in equity to finance the deal. At the time, a number of real estate professionals felt that the company overpaid for its acquisition. Flash ahead a couple of years, and you can see the Macklowe purchased the property at a bargain price at the bottom of the commercial real estate cycle, since the U.S. was leaving the recession after the Internet meltdown in 2001. The value of the property soared, like all assets, between 2003 and 2007. Some people estimated that the GM building was worth an astonishing $3.5 billion in 2007. Bankers were lining up to offer Macklowe financing based on the new value of the property.

In February 2007, Blackstone Group purchased the portfolio of class A properties from legendary investor Sam Zell's Equity Office Properties for $39 billion ($23 billion in cash and $16 billion in assumed debt). At the time, almost all commercial real estate investors felt that Blackstone Group had paid the absolute peak price for the cycle for this portfolio. Even Sam Zell could not see how this deal could make money for Blackstone Group, but he was smart enough to take the money and run. What no one had figured out was that Blackstone had a different way to play this deal. It never wanted to own most of the properties; it just wanted to make a few dollars. Like many before, it realized if it bought in bulk and resold it in smaller pieces that the sum of the pieces would be greater than the bulk price. Within days of closing the deal, it had deals to sell many of the truly unique properties to investors around the globe. It was able to sell so many buildings at premium prices that it paid for the deal and got a number of remaining buildings technically for free.

Once the Blackstone Equity office properties deal was closed, Blackstone approached Macklowe Properties to see if it was interested in purchasing some of the trophy buildings in the new Blackstone portfolio in the New York market. Macklowe jumped at the opportunity to be able to purchase some of these properties that rarely come up for sale, especially in bulk. Macklowe Properties purchased eight buildings representing 6.6 million square feet for $7 billion dollars ($100 million in equity and $6.9 billion in debt), an average price of $1,060 per square foot. To be able to afford the purchase, Macklowe had to pledge the newly purchased properties plus his world famous GM building as collateral for the loan. It was rumored that Macklowe was looking to flip some of the new properties at a higher price and then refinance the remaining portfolio long term. Unfortunately, the market moved against him. With the credit crisis starting, banks and other investors were hesitant to take on the risk of this highly leveraged deal, especially since the properties were purchased at peak cycle pricing.

The shutting down of the refinancing markets due to the credit crisis left Macklowe with few options. In May 2008, Macklowe sold the GM build-ing and three additional class A properties for $3.95 billion to Mortimer Zuckerman, CEO of Boston Properties, another large, world-famous proper-ty investor. The sale allowed Macklowe to pay down some of his short-term debt that was coming due from the Blackstone acquisition. This allowed the company some financial breathing space but cost it its most famous build-ing, the GM building. Before the deal to buy the 6.6 million square feet from the Blackstone Group, Macklowe owned or managed 10 million square feet. After the Blackstone purchase, it shot up to almost 17 million square feet. Now it is back to where it started. It is unclear if it now has more debt or if it is better off from the purchase. I would speculate the company is worse off, maybe not financially, but mentally, because it is a big blow to have to have to sell the best property in order to keep other properties of lesser prestige; while still class A, they are not as world famous as the GM building. I know if it was me, I would never have my driver drive by that building again, especially if I were the one who helped make it the great building that it is today. The pain would be too unbearable.

If Macklowe had waited two or three years, he could have bought a lot of the properties at a fraction of the price. He could have pulled off a repeat of the brilliant market move in acquiring the GM building at the bottom of the cycle in 2003. Alas, it is easy to armchair quarterback and second-guess a great property-investing company like Macklowe Properties. Sometimes it can even be therapeutic when you yourself are going through difficult times, like many are in the Western world. With the benefit of hindsight, I can easily say that the company took on too much leverage at a time of peak market prices. This has historically been the recipe of failure for many a prominent company.

I, too, cannot talk much. I have taken my profits from my consulting business and bought three small commercial properties with the thought that they would provide a stable income to offset my erratic consulting income. I purchased a couple of the properties at peak cycle prices in a declining market in areas that I probably would not have purchased today if I had to do it again. The properties were, at best, 7.5 cap properties (properties that would produce a 7.5% return after expenses but before cost of mortgage). If I had to do it today, I would have waited for properties in better locations at reasonable prices. I was caught up in the false assumption that a low and steady return today can make for something big in the future.

All this said, Macklowe and I are similar: we both took on some calculated risks in an effort to improve our commercial real estate portfolios. Most likely, our goals were to build larger portfolios that would provide future economic benefits. Unfortunately, we used faulty assumptions about the market and, in the case of Macklowe, a false assumption about the ability to refinance a large short-term debt easily. Both of these faults happen frequently to many businesses, the key here is to minimize your downside exposure to both market risk and financing risk where you can. Sometimes it is unavoidable, but most times a more conservative approach will help you achieve the companies' goals in the long-run without missing too many opportunities. Remember running a business is like a marathon not a sprint race, learn to strategically pace yourself. I now know better, I hope Macklowe has now learned that as well.

General Motors

"What's good for the country is good for General Motors, and vice versa" is a quote attributed to former GM President Charles Wilson. General Motors was the company that was the epitome of U.S. industrial companies in the 1950s and 1960s. The quote really harks back to how large and entwined General Motors was with the U.S. economy. At one point, some even thought General Motors was *the* U.S. economy. In the 1950s and 1960s, GM had market shares of the U.S. auto industry of around 50%. It was the largest and strongest financially of any company in the U.S. in its heyday. That was before the fuel crisis of the 1970s.

In the early '70s, all U.S. automakers were making bigger and more powerful cars to cater to the baby boomers' wants. There was a horsepower war that started in 1964 with the introduction of the GTO. This war was to capture headlines with who can make the fastest cars. It was seen as a very important marketing tool to help the automakers sell more vehicles. Elsewhere in the world, the Japanese and German automakers were building smaller, fun-to-drive cars with better fuel mileage. The large U.S. automakers were only concerned with the other U.S. automakers. They were not paying attention to the worldwide automakers when a geopolitical inflection point occurred.

In October 1973, OPEC members agreed to an oil embargo to retaliate for the U.S. supplying military arms to Israel after the start of Yom Kippur war. The Arab nations were upset that the U.S. was secretly supplying the

Israelis to help them defend lands taken during the 1967 Six Day war with Egypt. OPEC instituted a 25% output reduction with a further 5% additional reduction being threatened. In addition, the early '70s saw the start of world-wide inflation brought on by looser monetary policy following the Bretton Woods decision to take the U.S. off the gold exchange standard and debase its currency. This brought instant inflation to the Arab nations because oil is traded in U.S. dollars. The embargo caused the cost of a barrel of oil to jump from $3 to $12 per barrel almost overnight. That is the equivalent to oil jumping from $70 today to $280 in a matter of days.

Americans who drove big thirsty cars that got six to ten miles per gallon were in a state of shock. They were accustomed to buying gasoline at $0.25 to $0.35 per gallon. Gas increased to over $0.55 per gallon by June 1974. In space of less than a year, the price of gas increased by approximately 65%. Now that supplies were reduced, gas was being rationed because on most days up to 20% of the nation's gas stations had no gas to sell. The U.S. government had to deploy a rationing method, where an even license plate number or an odd license plate number determined which day you could fill up. Long lines formed at gas stations that did have fuel. People naturally changed their habits to deal with the changed environment. They started to drive less and carpool more in an effort to reduce the amount they spent on gas. They also stopped looking at oversized, greedy, gas-guzzling American cars and started buying thrifty, gas-sipping foreign cars.

General Motors was caught out with the wrong products in the market. It couldn't **give** away its cars, and thus the market share started to fall. This continued throughout the '70s and '80s. It repeatedly tried to build smaller, fuel-efficient cars but was continuously met with ho hum acceptance by U.S. auto buyers. Going from a market share approaching 50% to less than 30% left GM with a lot of spare capacity that had huge fixed costs. Couple that with increased pay demands, due to higher inflation, from the unions representing its workforce, GM experienced severe constraints with its balance sheet. It had multiple years of losses and negative cash flow where it had to borrow to meet its cash needs. Starting in the 1990s and 2000s, in order to move merchandise, GM had to resort to offering extremely favorable financing to provide incentive for people to purchase its products. This led to more and more debt being added annually to GM's balance sheet. When GM experienced good years, it only slightly decreased its use of debt. Instead of paying down large chunks of debt, it would reward shareholders with larger dividends, acquisitions, and share buybacks. By now, you should be starting to see a pattern here. When things are going good, the company spends the money it is making, and when they are going bad, it borrows money and pretends that times are good. A company can only do this for so long before it catches up to it.

This short-term thinking, coupled with the fact that the company was not watching its competitors or balance sheet, led GM to experience an out-of-control spiraling of its debt levels. If you combine this with the fact that it had an expensive labor force, inept management, and poorly received products, you can see why, in 2009, it had to finally file for bankruptcy protection. It was rumored to be close to possibly doing this in the early 1990s but was rescued by the ability to sell trucks and SUVs at large margins to baby boomers. I would argue that the writing was on the wall starting as early as the late 1980s that it was going to have to file bankruptcy some time. If you look at the cash flow statement, starting the mid-1980s, the company routinely reported that it was more becoming of a bank where cash flow from the business was less than its capital investment; its only way to grow was by increasing its financial portion of the equation. Most of the revenue growth was tied to growing the debt, similar to the large investment banks that got into trouble in the late 2000s.

Going back to the quote that I opened this section on, GM was very symbolic of the U.S. economy, but all the outward appearance of success was mostly an illusion in finance. If GM could not continuously offer favorable financing or take on more debt, it would have failed. This is similar to what the average U.S. household did in the 2000s. Even though people's income levels stayed static in real terms from 2001 to 2009, they took on more and more debt with the assumption that it was a time of prosperity.

The U.S. government is doing the exact same thing today. I strongly feel that in the future we will have a government debt financing problem.

General Motor's problems with debt are very different than the problems that Macklowe Properties experienced. Macklowe used debt to take a calculated risk to grow his business, which ultimately failed, but General Motors used debt to mask structural weaknesses in its operations. Macklowe operated his properties in a true world-class standard and is seen as an excellent property owner. General Motors was a failing company for almost four decades and used debt and its balance sheet to prolong the inevitable bankruptcy, hoping all along that something or someone would come along and save it.

Lesson to Learn From This Chapter

The lesson from this chapter is one of moderation. Leverage is best in moderation. Just because Wall Street is acting like a pusher offering addicting drugs at almost free rates doesn't mean they have your best interest in mind. They are trying to get you addicted to using their product, debt. If Wall Street is giving low interest rates, make sure the project has a large margin of safety and a high chance of success. Just borrowing to buy stock at peak prices or real estate at cap rates so low that Treasury bonds are better investments never makes sense even if you hold the stock or property for twenty years. Just wait a couple of years, and the market will change. All the companies and individuals that could not buy enough of the assets at peak prices will soon be paying you to take it off their hands at prices approaching 50% discounts or more. During the inevitable market declines, the sellers are not selling because they lost their minds or they somehow feel the need to be nice to strangers; they are selling because they cannot afford the leverage they took on to buy the asset in the peak market. By waiting, you leverage your dollars because you are buying at a large discount.

Some people reading this chapter might think that I am against deploying leverage. That could not be further from the truth. I believe that if a business or individual deploys leverage in small but timely doses, it will improve the overall result, provided they use it to invest in assets and projects that produce returns greater than the cost of capital. Deploying leverage to buy assets at peak prices just because the interest rate is cheap or to buy back shares to improve quarterly results are always things that come back and bite you in the ass down the road. Even if such things do not impact your results negatively in the short term, they will impact your access to cash right when you could use it most. At that time, you are like the other 95% of the companies in the world, bitching, "Woe is me. If only I had funding, I would love to be buying such-and-such asset or company right now." If you are smart enough to have cash and a strong balance sheet, you can and probably do demand extremely favorable pricing at times when the market is dropping.

CHAPTER 16

Yes, Virginia, There is an Ebenezer Scrooge!

I want to start this chapter off by stating I personally do not like Christmas. I do not like the cold weather, the over-commercialization, the forced getting together with people that you typically only see once a year for a reason, and all the false happiness and fakeness that this season seems to bring out in the common man. I do love the look of surprise and amazement on my children's faces when they get to open all their loot. I love the time off. I love the Christmas parties where companies let their hair down for a bit and allow their employees to drink too much and party too hard (you know who you are!) all on the company dime. What's not to love about free food and booze?

To some, the company Christmas party has become **the** company party of the year, something to look forward to in an otherwise bleak and boring work environment. That is why the next quote from one of my clients is so shocking. During the second week of October, as usual, the executive secretary announced to the company to reserve the evening of the second Saturday in December for the annual company Christmas party. Without looking at the calendar, they somehow did not realize that the same date was the date of the town's annual Christmas lights parade, which everyone in the town turned out to attend. The company probably chose this day to save money since the town offered only limited venues for decent-sized Christmas parties. All the hotels and large restaurants were probably wide open without a single reservation because everyone knew about the parade—everyone, that is, except the company. Immediately, a lot of the employees complained. A couple of weeks later, the company decided to change the date to the week before, presumably since all the rest of the days were already booked solid.

The company sent out an announcement notifying everyone of the change and also telling them of a new benefit. Every year since the dawn of time (or at least 1980, whichever came first), the company would give every employee a voucher at a local grocery store to either purchase a turkey or a ham for the season. This year, to make up for the change in dates, the company decided to seem extra charitable; it offered to allow employees to donate their vouchers to one of three different charities (local food bank, homeless shelter, or Salvation Army), and it would match the gift. This was a brilliant idea and was widely looked upon favorably by the employees. The company looked like it was truly giving back to the community.

Then, the next day, the employees got the following email from the CEO.

To All Employees,

We are experiencing a severely diminished economic climate where most companies are trying to maximize their effectiveness within their industries. A decision has been made that the company will no longer subsidize any non-commercial spending. Unfortunately, this includes all spending on Christmas parties and non-business-producing activities across the company.

Regards,
CEO (Name withheld so as not to cause the CEO to be besieged with hate mail)

So the company had canceled Christmas! Really? Christmas! The fact that it came so shortly after the original announcement made matters worse. It would have been better off never announcing anything in the first place. The employees took this like they should, as a slap in the face. Society has taboos. One of the main taboos is canceling Christmas. As one who clearly does not like Christmas, even I know not to cancel Christmas.

The reason for canceling Christmas got even more controversial, looking at the company's numbers. Due to the tough economic conditions, the company's revenue and profits did not grow the year they canceled Christmas. While other companies' revenues and profits were sinking, this company was able to maintain flat revenue and only a slight decrease in profits. The reason they canceled Christmas was that the company was behind on hitting its forecasted revenue and profit numbers (unrealistic numbers that still had them growing at double digits rates even while the rest of the industry was falling by double digits). The roughly $25K in cost for the Christmas event would have been a rounding error on the company's books. The fact that the company was holding its own was of no consequence to the board. They wanted the revenue and profit number to hit what was quoted to Wall Street and did not care what the company did to make it. The greedy buggers!

As can be imagined, morale sank through the floor. This was the last straw. This extreme short-sightedness took years to live down. It became folklore at the company as "the year that the company canceled Christmas." I honestly would not be surprised if this action made the local and national news. I know times are tough during the Great Recession, but this is a step too far. I can see the headlines now: "The Ebenezer Scrooge of the 21st Century." Talk about a potential public relations nightmare.

To make matters even worse, the company did not continue the free turkey and ham tradition. That meant that three deserving charities also had to do without. The homeless and the starving had to tighten their belts a little more in this season of giving. Talk about a 180-degree change, where the company was looking to help, but now the company was taking food out of their mouths. In fairness to the CEO, the company did wind up offering a small potluck lunch (during company time, mind you) in early December, but the damage was already done.

I once worked for a company that was circling the drain toward bankruptcy and it did not even cancel Christmas. Instead of spending the $30K to $40K that it normally did every year so that all employees could attend one big shindig, it decided to give all the small teams of employees a couple of hundred dollars and an afternoon off to have smaller parties at local restaurants or pubs. The employees understood why they did not have a big party because the company could not afford it. In fact, a lot of the employees chipped in to help make their reduced Christmas parties truly fun events.

Lesson to Learn From This Chapter

I can sum up the lesson in four words: "Never ever cancel Christmas." There are some things you never do in business unless your back is against the wall. It is understandable to reduce your spending in times of need-- that is the prudent thing to do--but when things are not really that bad, do not let the pursuit of short-term profits affect your long-term success. Somewhere there is a Wall Street tycoon who is licking his lips for me to reveal the CEO's name so that he can hire him or her to run one of the leveraged buyout (LBO)companies so he make even more money. I now sound a little like Michael Moore bringing this up, but to me this is being majorly cheap. As I have said in the past, I am a major believer in capitalism, but this is where profit over all is clearly wrong and the company crossed some invisible line that should never be breached with its employees if it wants to be around longer than a year.

Conclusion

I truly had fun writing this book. It allowed me to bring up fond memories of working with great people at poorly run companies throughout the years. I have always felt that we learn better from our mistakes because of the pain they bring firsthand. Our memories tell us to proceed cautiously when we see a similar situation. In business, it is a little different. Instead of doing something that might cost you some embarrassment or physical pain, a mistake can cost you your capital, job, and possibly your future. If you can look at other people's mistakes and learn from them, you can learn the lesson without the pain to your wallet or wellbeing. And that is why it is important to learn what not to do in business.